WELCOME TO REPLICA DODGE

WELCOME TO REPLICA DODGE

A MEMOIR BY

NATALIE RUTH JOYNTON

Illustrated By Emily Joynton

Wayne State University Press
Detroit

Made in Michigan Writers Series

General Editors

Michael Delp, Interlochen Center for the Arts
M. L. Liebler, Wayne State University

A complete listing of the books in this series can be found online at wsupress.wayne.edu

---

ISBN 978-0-8143-4557-3 (paperback)
ISBN 978-0-8143-4558-0 (e-book)

Library of Congress Control Number: 2018957219

Publication of this book was made possible by a generous gift from The Meijer Foundation. This work is supported in part by an award from the Michigan Council for Arts and Cultural Affairs.

Wayne State University Press
Leonard N. Simons Building
4809 Woodward Avenue
Detroit, Michigan 48201–1309

Visit us online at wsupress.wayne.edu

Advance praise for *Welcome to Replica Dodge*

"Authentic, fresh, pragmatic and profound, this gem of a memoir knits a vivid sense of place with a deeply spiritual journey. Book clubs will find a bright, witty voice, a pitch-perfect story, and fertile ground for discussion. I look forward to hearing more from this talented author."

—Joni Rodgers, *New York Times* bestselling author of *Bald in the Land of Big Hair*

"Like the best nonfiction, *Welcome to Replica Dodge* is about many things—place and displacement, house and home, idealism and identity, religious conversion and self-reliance—and the elements all combine to create an evocative, thoughtful, wonderfully entertaining memoir that I can't recommend highly enough."

— Porter Shreve, author of *The End of the Book*

"Natalie Ruth Joynton has written a page-turning delight—funny, tender, and smart. Joynton discovers Jewishness, romance, family history, a remote corner of Michigan, and her own future, and most remarkably she makes you feel that you're with her every step of the way. This book is a joy, both poignant and vital."

—David Mikics, author of *Bellow's People*

"*Welcome to Replica Dodge* is more than a memoir, it's an homage to place and finding your position in it. Joynton takes us through her journey of making a home in the wilds of Michigan, and offers us intimacy with place, and making peace with the past. In her honest, openhearted prose, Joynton examines her conversion and life as a Jew in the Midwest, and with her powers of observation and compassion, she in turn gives us a new pioneer narrative. This is a book about making a home in the most unexpected places. How Joynton subverts the stranger in a strange land narrative is remarkable. Joynton's compassion and warmth is on every page, as she recounts her inventive spirit in rural America. A smart and insightful debut."

—Nina McConigley, author of *Cowboys and East Indians*, winner of the PEN Open Book Award

For my mom,
Patricia Ann,
who wrote down my stories
before I could write

CONTENTS

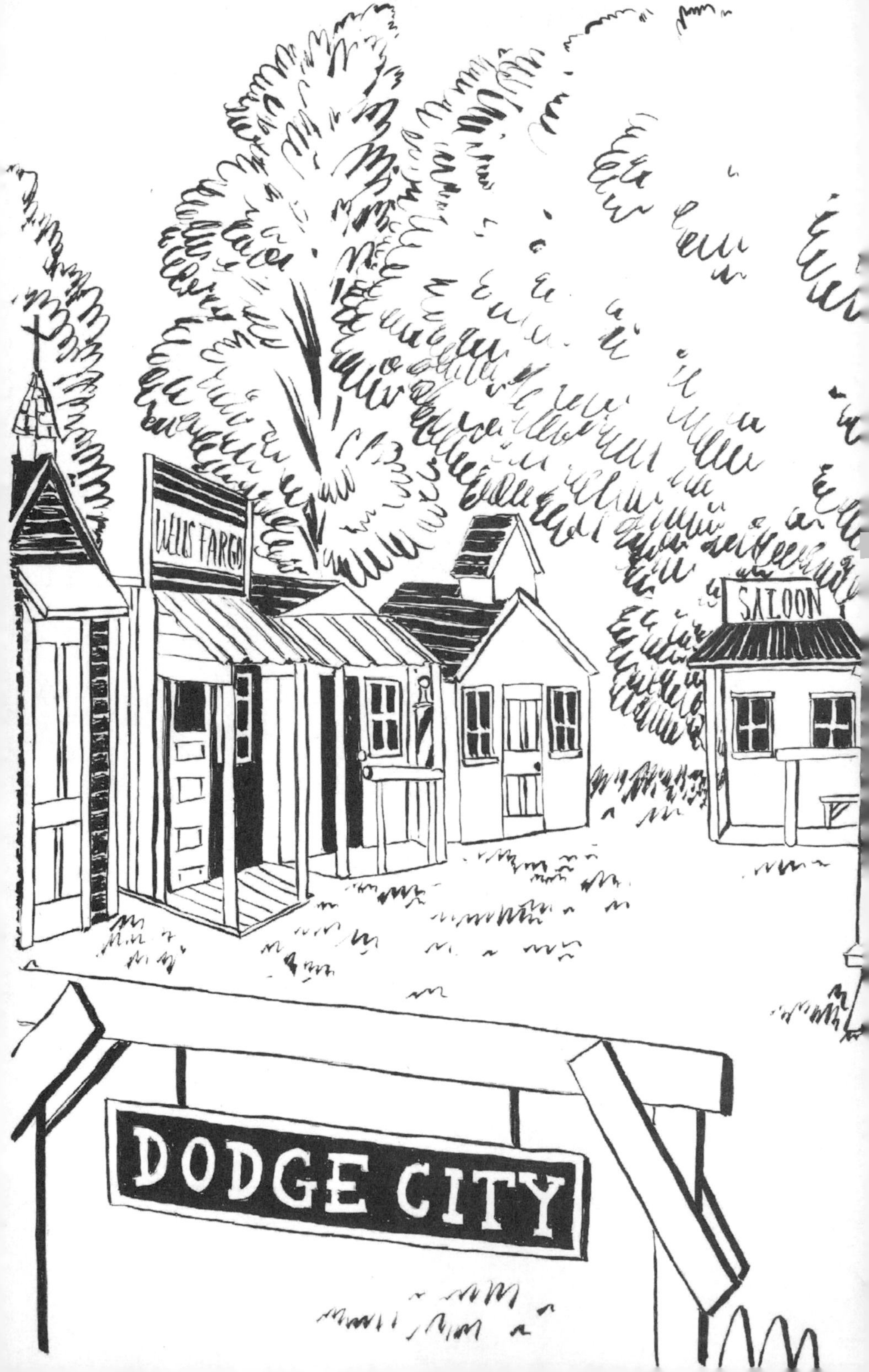
WELLS FARGO
SALOON
DODGE CITY

BAT MASTE[R]

REPLICA DODGE

AUTHOR'S NOTE

MEMORY IS POWERFUL and informative, singular and selective. In writing this book I often wrestled with my own imperfect sense of the past. *Did it really happen like that? Am I remembering this just as it occurred?* While my awareness of the limits of memory has guided me as a writer, this narrative should not be read as unbiased fact. In the end, *Welcome to Replica Dodge* is just one person's true story.

Most names have been changed to protect the privacy of those involved.

1

REPLICA DODGE

ANY OTHER REAL estate agent but Pam would've given up on us. What we thought we wanted—or what I'd been looking for—didn't exist in rural Mason County, Michigan, and as frank as she was about flooring and bankers, Pam let me sort out this suspended disbelief in my own time. She was a straightforward woman who, I'd heard, inseminated her own cows, and for months she'd stuck with us as we started our search with newer homes in Ludington but ended up asking to see properties further inland, deep in the countryside, in the tight low hills owned mostly by farmers and hemmed in by great swaths of hardwoods.

Then on one evening in early April, Pam took us to Replica Dodge.

By now our search for a new house had dragged on for almost a year. The days were still cold enough to require a jacket and gloves, and my breath hung right in front of my face. We were fifteen miles inland from the small town of Ludington, set along the Lake Michigan coast, when we pulled into the driveway off a thin dirt road. Replica Dodge included four acres, a large white farmhouse, and a red barn, all situated across from the most expansive cherry orchard I'd ever seen. It was our first time visiting the property we'd eventually buy, but that night as Pam ushered us toward the house, I stood outside wearing my bafflement as a blank stare. We had visited over twenty places for sale in Mason County, but neither of us had ever seen anything like this.

Joe looked at me and I looked at him.

"Don't worry," Pam said as she steered us toward the front door. "You can tear all that down."

I squinted in the fading light. What was *that*?

At first the buildings in the front yard struck me as the film set for a western. Not the real West but the mythic one, shown late at night on television for people who can't sleep. Black-and-white reels that open with the high whine of an orchestra, tumbleweeds swept up on a strong wind, endless miles of parched earth. Only this was orchard country. This was Michigan with its motto: *If you seek a pleasant peninsula, look about you.*

Yet what stood before us seemed straight out of that myth. Situated in a semicircle in the front yard, facing the house rather than the road, were nine buildings: a saloon, a bank, a church, a barbershop, a one-room schoolhouse, a general store, a jailhouse, a bunkhouse, and one "Lady's Emporium." Crafted of barn wood and capped with steel roofs, each seemed big enough to walk into—could we go inside?—I asked. Above it all loomed a sign that read *Dodge City.*

"I'd strip everything, sell the antiques," Pam called over her shoulder. Then she turned to us. "Why don't you come inside the house?"

I headed instead toward the spectacle. Joe followed. Together we stepped into Replica Dodge's church, where we were immediately surrounded by dozens of antiques, befitting heirlooms of the real Dodge City's heyday. They had been painstakingly arranged.

"Bizarre," Joe whispered.

I nodded but had no words for what I was looking at. A church in miniature, just the right size for two or three worshippers. On a small wooden pew before us were three hymnals lying open to the same song. I ran my fingers over one's thin page, "Battle Hymn of the Republic." I stared but did not pick them up. There was something eerie about the careful way they'd been placed, as if the few congregants had, only moments before, risen in the rapture foretold by the lyrics.

Mine eyes have seen the glory of the coming of the Lord.

Disoriented, we moved on to Replica Dodge's bank, where we found a Marcel typewriter, its ink tape still intact. I pressed down the Q and watched the sticky key rise back into position. In the barbershop an old-fashioned barber chair faced a mounted mirror, its porcelain frame like ice to the touch. Someone had draped a long leather strap over the arm of the chair, and for the second time the intentional, uncanny nature of Replica Dodge struck me. It was as if the barber had just finished sharpening his razor, rinsed out his horsehair brush, and closed up shop for the day.

Walking through Replica Dodge was like walking through a cemetery. The whole place discouraged speech, but two questions beat through me. What was this place? Who built it?

I didn't know then what I know now of Replica Dodge— the name we coined that evening for the property that would soon be ours—and I hadn't yet met Bill Broadwell, owner and inventor of the oddity. That night we just stared, exiting one building and entering another. We turned over the antiques: the saloon's ancient liquor bottles, the bunkhouse's traveling trunks. Neither of us knew what to say. Everything was heavier in my hands than expected.

☾

THAT'S HOW THE prospect of staying in Mason County felt to me. Heavy.

Not just heavy—unwieldy. Like I had strapped a pack on my back whose contents were breakable and precious, and I had just hiked into the wilderness with no map. This sense left me calculating how long I would have to go before I could sit down and rest. How many steps did I need to take here? How long did we *really* need to stay?

This sense was also why it had taken us almost a year to find a place, and by then, like anyone shouldering such a burden, I was eager for distraction. Enter Replica Dodge. By the end of April, we had made our first offer on the property, and I busied myself mastering a brief history of the real Dodge City, Kansas, a place I'd never been. Its nicknames were as strange as the town situated in our future front lawn: Cowboy Capital, Queen of the Cowtowns, and the most notable, Beautiful, Bibulous Babylon of the Frontier.

I learned that the real Dodge City was established in 1872 and had served as a commercial intersection of the Old West. It was where buyers of cattle met herds driven up from the south, often from Texas. Texas was where I'd been born and raised, my first home, and coming across this piece of trivia made me smile. I kept doing that—ferreting out even the smallest connections—as we prepared to purchase Replica Dodge.

Much has been said of the wickedness and unrighteousness of the city, one article written in 1878 for the *Kinsley Graphic* read. *There is but one difference, however, which is a frontier characteristic: our neighbors do not pretend to hide their peculiarities.*

Not pretending to hide peculiarities seemed a sufficient way to describe whoever built Replica Dodge in their front yard. No, I stopped myself. *Our* front yard. I wondered again about its creator, this person who had erected a tribute to the West in a state famous for its fresh water. Why had they built it? Why hadn't they simply gone west, to the real Dodge City?

We met Bill Broadwell in Ludington three weeks later for the house signing. It was May and the days were getting longer, the lake less ferocious. From inside the agency, sandwiched between Pam and Joe, I watched Bill climb out of his Buick. My heart sank. Bill was in his eighties, a full-bellied man leaning hard against a black cane. Joe got up to open the door for him. Bill was no longer capable of maintaining his creation.

Between the shuffling and signing of endless documents, he answered some of my questions about Replica Dodge. After retiring from the auto business in 1995, Bill had moved to Mason County, bought the four acres, tore down its rambling chicken coop, and set to work on his retirement project: reconstructing the "Wickedest Little City in America" in the front lawn of his Michigan homestead.

The bigger question—*why* he had built it—I would never get fully answered. As Pam doled out the paperwork and I tried not to think about the fact that I was now legally bound to Mason County, I listened to Bill speak of the place with such affection that it became clear that he didn't want to move. Given the option, Bill would die at Replica Dodge.

A flicker of shame shot through me. I was dragging my feet about staying somewhere others deemed heaven on earth and here was Bill, the old soothsayer, wagging his finger in my direction. With its miles of blue coast, bounty of fresh fruit, endless fields and farm stands, white Christmases and sap season, in many ways Mason County, Michigan, was Eden. Even so, it wasn't my paradise.

At the end of the signing I asked Bill point-blank why he'd built Replica Dodge.

The old man shrugged. "I always wanted my own city."

The room got quiet. Bill looked away from me. I took the cue and also looked away, studying the slew of papers spread between us. It occurred to me then why Replica Dodge faced the farmhouse rather than the road. It wasn't for the passerby's gratification. It was Bill's city, his version of home. Bill had created what he couldn't, for whatever reason, reach in reality.

As Joe signed the final document passing ownership of Replica Dodge on to us, I fought a strong urge to run. Out of the room, out of Mason County, out of the state. Instead I focused on Bill's right hand, which lay folded over an old tattoo on his left forearm. It was a pinup girl, 1950s-style bikini and bouffant hair, but her sharp curves had thickened so much with age, and she was blurred so far into Bill's skin, that it was hard, at first, to tell what she was.

☾

ON THE NIGHT of our first visit to Replica Dodge, we discovered the schoolhouse contained the fewest heirlooms. On a shelf sat some Merrill readers enveloped in dust. When I opened one, a yellowed receipt fell out onto the floor. Joe picked it up and handed it to me. "I think they were using it as a bookmark."

"Apron," I read. "March 7, 1909. Seventy-nine cents."

Above the schoolhouse chalkboard, Bill had framed a list of rules for teachers from some "1917 Coal Mine Board of Education," whatever that was. Joe read them out loud: "You must wear at least two petticoats." We shared a nervous laugh. "You may not loiter downtown in the ice cream store."

As the last pink light snagged through the sky we entered Replica Dodge's general store. The buildings were getting darker and less believable, and we squinted at the stockpile of antiques lining the store's walls: Red Dot gunpowder, Ranger saddles, seasoned cast iron skillets, a cash register with a bell that chimed when the drawer flew open with a bang. In the jailhouse, a rocking chair sat beside a parlor stove. A gun lay across the marshal's desk.

Maybe that's when I knew we would buy the property, even before we saw the farmhouse or barn. Joe accepted Replica Dodge but was motivated more by the recent twenty-thousand-dollar cut on the asking price. The property had been on the market for a long time, though what impressed Joe most was the land itself, its series of slight hills and slow dips, the thin strip of hardwoods, the giant black walnut trees hanging over the drive. At four acres, Replica Dodge was big enough for hobby farming but still small enough that no industrial farming equipment was needed, and that night, by the end of our visit, Joe had identified at least four types of fruit growing there: currants, apples, peaches, and grapes. For Joe, the place offered just enough room to grow a garden, keep chickens and some goats, maybe even start a family.

But something deeper drew me to Replica Dodge. Beyond its heirlooms and Bill's craftsmanship, beyond even the grand distraction it provided me as I made some of the biggest decisions of my young life yet, claiming Joe as my mate and, by extension, accepting that we would stay in Mason County, at least for a little while. All of these things mattered, but not as much as the plain fact that like me, Replica Dodge was out of place. Supremely.

As a mock western ghost town in the middle of Michigan, Replica Dodge made about as much sense as me calling Mason County home. In this dependable landscape where every season looked exactly as expected—as if Norman Rockwell was stationed right outside, painting away—Replica Dodge was foreign, and I recognized that kinship. It was the Jewish part of me that would never celebrate Christmas, and the Texan in me who would always hate a winter coat. Replica Dodge was the architectural manifestation of life as I suddenly now knew it, existing as one piece of the greater environment that didn't quite fit.

And yet the city stood.

2

BODY AND SOUL

In Judaism there's a word used to describe a specific kind of divine mix-up or mistake. The word translates from Hebrew to mean someone born Jewish to a Christian family, raised in the church rather than the synagogue, but it's different from the word for convert (*ger*).

Someone said it to me once, a young man standing outside the Hillel building on the University of Houston campus. I was a sophomore in college. Though kind, the man refused to shake my hand. He wore a plain black suit, a white shirt, and a small head covering over his dark curls.

I've lost that word, but I'll always remember what he said right after he rattled it off. "Of course, the highest task of that person is to find their way back home."

Home. Say it aloud and it's the shape your mouth makes at the start of a yawn.

Warm, idiosyncratic, *home* haunts our American idioms: *Home sweet home, You can never go home, Home is where the heart is*, yet as soon as one begins to define it, it changes. The word's chameleonic character means it has the power to encompass both objects and people, slip from cities to siblings, exist in life's holiest moments but also pop up within our most common rituals. *Home* is the word people getting married say at the ceremony, some form of "I've found a home in you." High and low, home can be the green light of a cheap coffee maker or the person one chooses to love. At best, it's where we are safe and belong.

But even when a home is shared, one's version of it remains a singular experience. This is why close siblings often recall their childhood home in different terms. One sister remembers the aroma of the kitchen (curry and ginger), while another evokes the house's oddities (that last missing step leading down to the basement floor).

Still others think more broadly, home as a stretch of land or an entire city. Or one's family, fixed forever at a certain age in a snapshot of memory. As a girl I remember bouncing on my father's knee, counting the six colors of his beard—brown, red, black, gray, blond, and white strands—all mixed together. Somehow that still feels like home to me.

The tricky part of course, is that I'm remembering him at forty-four. Now he's heading toward seventy. For most of us, home is a distant and unreachable place, or at least there is the home of the past and the home of today.

The second letter of the Hebrew alphabet (*bet*) means "house." *Beit Yisrael*, house of Israel, and *Beth-El*, house of God, are both derivatives and frequent names of American synagogues. The same derivative constitutes *bet din*, a rabbinical court, or what is referred to in Judaism as the house of the judges.

I was in my final semester as a graduate student at Purdue University when I drove to Indianapolis to face a bet din. After five years of study and observance, I had done exactly what that young man years before had hinted at: I had found my way home, at least spiritually speaking. After passing the last examination—an extended conversation with two rabbis and a cantor—I braved the *mikveh*, a ritual bath made of rainwater. Only it was January in Indiana, so the bath was made of snow, not rain, which had been brought indoors and left to melt. My sponsoring rabbi warned me it would be cold but that I needed to immerse my whole body. I waded into it naked. I completed my conversion to Judaism.

I wish I could remember that word for those born Jewish to Christian families. The idea that the body comes from one place, but the soul arrives from another. That each child is born part mother, part father, but also something else entirely. That sometimes mix-ups happen. That the bright center ablaze in each of us belongs to no one. I still believe in this notion, because during the final segment of my conversion ceremony, the last moment before I became officially Jewish, something strange happened.

I began to cough. A lot. I wasn't sick but by my final pledge, my coughing had crescendoed into a hacking fit. The judges exchanged glances, unsure of what to do as I went red in the face. I tried to catch my breath and reel in my embarrassment. Finally Joe, pressed into a corner of that small room, asked if I needed a drink. He gave me a bottle of water.

Then the rabbi stopped, mid-blessing. "Are you alright?" she asked.

Good question. At the time, I didn't know. I took another long sip of the water, but it only made the sudden affliction worse, so I stood there coughing out the remainder of my pledge, as if some Southern Baptist was crawling up my throat, cueing up "This Little Light of Mine." As if my whole family had just walked in and caught me facing the bet din of Indianapolis.

Of my own free will I have chosen to become a Jew—cough!

I will practice Judaism to the exclusion—cough cough!—*of all other religions.*

If blessed—cough!—*with children*—cough!—*I will rear them as Jews.*

☾

I GREW UP north of Houston, between I-610's loop around downtown and the beginning of Angus cattle country. Between the Rothko Museum, the Houston Ballet, and the Huntsville State Prison, not an hour further north, where rumor had it more executions happened annually in the 1990s than anywhere else in America. In that suburban middle my childhood was littered with strip malls: Rudy's barbershop, Blockbuster Video, Starbucks, tanning salons, Staples, and one single arboretum, where the koi would eat from my hand.

People not from Houston see the city as a good ol' boys' oil town, and some of that attitude persists, but for decades now, Houston's biggest market has been medical research and care. The city is also far less conservative than most outsiders assume. In 2009 Houstonians elected Annise Parker, one of the first openly gay mayors of any major U.S. city (since then they've reelected her twice), and according to the 2013 census, Houston, with almost 2.2 million residents, recently outranked New York City in ethnic and racial diversity. This is why there's hardly a hint of a southern drawl to my voice. ("You're from Texas?" my Michigan students ask. "Where's your accent?")

You should understand that these endorsements are exactly what a native Houstonian would do. We see it as our job to defend the city against its narrower stereotypes. Phillip Lopate, a Brooklyn-born essayist, once described Houston as "a decentralized octopus gobbling up all the land around it," and that much is true. It is difficult, traveling north of Houston, to note exactly where the city ends and the suburbs where I grew up begin.

Like many of the other middle-class neighborhoods in Houston, Lexington Woods was full of the same three or four houses in various shades of beige, and there's still something about that place, and every suburb I've been to since, that's like standing between a waterfall and the cool slab of rock behind it. Like trying to live in a closed space between the impossibly loud and the incredibly thick.

My parents must have also felt fenced. Or they were never completely at home, because when I was a girl, our family made trips downtown each week after church. Me and my older sister Lauren in the back seat of our silver Lincoln Continental, my mother and father in front, all in our Sunday best. It was only a short drive before we were really in our element: Opera in the Heights, tuba recitals at Rice University, the Japanese Garden in Hermann Park Conservancy.

Though we lived in Houston's never-ending suburbs, cognitively, my parents tried to ensure that our family experienced life inside the loop, or at least they succeeded in letting us know that the suburbs weren't really where we belonged. My father was a philosophy professor; my mother transcribed doctor's notes in Houston's Medical Center, at the heart of downtown.

It worked, I know, because when I go back to Texas now, I have no desire to return to Lexington Woods. I'm at home among Cy Twombly's gigantic white paintings in the art district, or Rothko's darker, holier work a block down. I'm at home in the symphony hall, listening to the musicians warm up, or walking the sidewalks busted up by the roots of towering oaks, those trees that never cease flourishing in the city's inescapable heat, humidity, and sunlight.

☾

SHORTLY AFTER MY cough-riddled, bracingly cold formal welcome to Judaism, I graduated from Purdue and relocated to Ludington, Michigan, where Joe and I had secured teaching gigs at a small community college. They were the ultimate starter positions, and as adjunct faculty members, we subsisted a millimeter above the local poverty line of Mason County.

I was still young enough then (twenty-four) to believe that I'd someday return to Houston. That living anywhere else was some brief detour and I could, if bored, scurry back south. It was easy at first, that belief in returning, because there was nothing permanent tying us to Mason County. Like almost everyone we knew who was fresh out of college, Joe and I were struggling to navigate a job market caught in the collective sigh of the Great Recession.

And Michigan was beautiful—its white beaches nothing like the algae-spewing Texas Gulf I'd known as a kid—and Michigan was where we had met and where Joe had grown up (though on the Huron side, not the Lake Michigan shore). So we gave it a shot. Why not? Life on the lake sounded fine, at least for a little while. We rented a tiny cottage off Lake Michigan and began applying to full-time professorships both in and out of state, and it was around then we made a promise to each other: whoever got an offer first, the other would follow.

☾

WE WERE POST-COLLEGE poor, but life proved picturesque along Michigan's western lakeshore, at least until we learned that the cottage we were leasing had cheap rent because it was built for summer. Not winter. By November, the cottage's insulation was a joke that had lost its punch line. By December ice was building up on the roof. Freezing water began leaking into our bedroom. We spent a lot of time with our noses an inch away from the only heater in the kitchen. Finally to prevent further damming and leaking, Joe purchased two pairs of panty hose, stuffed the legs with deicer, and slung them over the side of the roof. For a while that winter, it looked like there were two nude women dozing near our chimney.

Still the people of Mason County extended themselves to us gently, almost unnoticeably, in that first year, in what I now know is emblematic of rural Michigan culture. When our rusted-out Mercedes Benz broke down, another professor at the college picked us up each morning, and even let us borrow his wheels on weekends to get groceries. There were dinner invitations from other faculty members who in kindness fed us lamb and steaks, warm brie and smoked salmon, delicacies we could never afford on our own.

At last a year later, a professional break came. For Joe. A full-time position opened at the community college where we worked and he was hired as the new tenure-track physics professor. And what followed, at first, was a resounding sense of relief.

Fiscally speaking, I'm not sure I could've stood another "big date" that meant ordering a single large pizza on payday. But in the months afterward, this emotion morphed from relief to surprise, doubt, and stalled out at disappointment. *So I'm the follower,* I kept thinking. For the first time I took a long look at where I'd unwittingly promised to stay. Mason County was not some post-college stopover where we'd ready ourselves for employment in some more exciting location. It was where we would live.

A few months later Joe proposed. It was the morning after Valentine's Day and I was teaching at the college, leading a class discussion on a student's paper that posited waterboarding as an ethical wartime tactic. Obviously love was in the air. Then Joe burst into my classroom with panicked determination.

I nearly panicked myself before he handed a camera to someone near the front, asked me to stand up, got down on one knee, and said many things I don't remember. He had been carrying the ring in his briefcase for weeks, four diamonds encircling a bright sapphire, blue and white like a prayer shawl. My students ate it up, but by the end I was more worried about the fact that Joe was squeezing me right where my thigh met my butt. Hard.

This is where our search for a new home began. Committed to one another and suddenly locals of Mason County, Michigan. The county's largest town, Ludington, rides the Lake Michigan coast and is not near any type of booming metropolis. Chicago is four and half hours south; Canada is to the north. The 2010 census recorded eight thousand residents of Ludington, but that number is misleading because each May the population burgeons when the *fudgies*, wealthy Chicagoans with vacation homes on Lakeshore Drive, flood the area and fill the fudge shops. Within certain local circles, I soon learned, these urban tourists are also referred to as FIPS or FOPS—Fucking Illinois People or Fucking Ohio People.

Mason County's population remains 96 percent white. When I began teaching at the community college, I was the only Jew I knew. When it came time to uphold my end of the bargain and stay in Mason County, these facts shifted from peculiar to deafening.

Sensing my apprehension, Joe suggested that we start the search for a house completely on my terms. Fine, I thought. Never mind that I wasn't in Texas anymore, not even in the South, I went foraging for any trace of my former life, or what I'd always assumed I could return to: some hot sprawling city, a thriving downtown art district, sidewalks cracked open by roots.

It took a long time for me to understand that replicating a former life in the urban South was unattainable, perhaps because on the surface, I almost could. As in Houston's Lexington Woods, the newer suburban homes in Ludington all shared an architectural sameness: open-floor plans and neutral-hued kitchens, flip-a-switch gas fireplaces, curb-less driveways, walls with built-in shelves for flat-screen televisions. But something kept us searching. Perhaps it was my ultimate refusal to rejoin anything that felt like the suburbs—even if it was the only thing that felt familiar in Mason County—or Joe's preference for acreage, or maybe it was finally dawning on me, with each new house showing in the small Michigan town, just how distant and unreachable my childhood was.

Six months into our year-long house hunt, we began making appointments for houses outside Ludington's limits. First single-acre properties, then farms. At eight months in, we were driving ten minutes east of town. My suspended disbelief carried on its fugue. The wooden houses became bigger, older, and further apart, the air loose and luffing like a sail over the asparagus fields.

19

Having worked for years to earn the trust of the Jewish community, having finally being recognized as one of them, I had promptly landed myself where there were no Jews.

And for what? I wondered. For love?

When did one person—one version of home—become worth another?

In those final weeks before purchasing Replica Dodge, I kept telling myself that nothing could change the fact that I was Jewish, but on a deeper level I was stenciling a return to urban life within ten years. It didn't need to be Houston anymore, I told myself. *Any city*, I repeated, *any city*. That's what I was thinking when we pulled into the driveway of Replica Dodge. This could still be a stopover, a long stopover, true, but a stopover.

In any case, wasn't I used to being spiritually alone?

3

A BRIEF TALE OF NOT TELLING

STRONG FAITH HAS a way of settling in after tragedy strikes. Mary Ruth Joynton, my grandmother and namesake, is really at the beginning of this story, as are her tragedies. She was one of the most committed Christians I've ever known, and like many women of the Deep South, Mary Ruth was called by both her first and middle names. She was a tall, dark-haired Louisiana Southern Baptist who was given, from time to time, to bouts of brutal honesty.

Once when I was a girl we were driving to the grocery store when she whipped around at a red light to reprimand me for saying "Gosh." She leaned over the middle console as far as she could into the back seat and said, her voice low and clipped, "You and I both know that's a stand-in for God." Mary Ruth's blue eyes were slits. "It's a grave and perilous sin, taking the Lord's name in vain. I pray you are forgiven, Natalie Ruth."

We drove on in silence.

I had inherited her middle name, Ruth, a name I started using in college as my first, though this was two years before my interest in Judaism began. I made the switch right after high school not because of my grandmother, but for the simple fact that I saw Ruth as a strong and uncommon name. It was somehow more fit for me—or the person I wanted to become—than Natalie, the feminine one my parents had given me at birth.

Mary Ruth was a child during the Depression. When she was a little girl living in Mississippi, her father swung off a rope into a river, split his leg open, and was lame for the rest of his life. Out of pain he took to what my grandmother referred to as "the drink," and when he died of alcoholism, my grandmother, as the eldest, abandoned her university studies to earn money for the family.

This is when her strong faith set in, but it was only Mary Ruth's first tragedy. At twenty-five she married my grandfather, Harry Joynton, a naval commander in charge of a destroyer in the years following World War II. Harry was kind and loyal, but military life meant that Mary Ruth was soon left alone for months at a stretch with their two young sons, in new home after new home, relocating every few years as they crisscrossed the country from California to Bethesda, Maryland. She never spent enough time anywhere to settle in, but my grandmother always found a church. On the harder days, my father remembers, she'd begin to sing an old standard.

Sometimes I feel like a motherless child
a long way from home.
Sometimes I feel
I'm almost gone.

Over a decade later, when Harry retired from the navy, Mary Ruth was finally free to use the English degree she'd completed with credits from six different colleges. They moved back to Louisiana, where she was hired as an English teacher by one of the poorest public schools in New Orleans. She claimed she loved that job, the children, and that she enjoyed her colleagues, but personal fulfillment proved a short-lived phenomenon for my grandmother. Soon after she started teaching, an active chapter of the Black Panthers surrounded the school, locked the children and staff inside, and demanded that the only white teacher leave the premises and never come back. It was the 1960s, the South, and Mary Ruth did as she was told.

One begins to understand the idea of being lifted up by the hand of Jesus.

☾

THREE WEEKS BEFORE my formal conversion to Judaism, Mary Ruth phoned. I could count on my grandmother, slick as an otter at play, weaving Christianity in and out of our conversations. She would remark on the annual fellowship luncheon fund-raiser (or the like) and then pause—always the tactical pauses—to see if I would share similar experiences. Conversing with Mary Ruth involved a roundabout spiritual checkup I had come to expect, but sometimes, during one of those bouts of brutal honesty, she'd dive deep. All of a sudden the play was off and the hunt was on. When she called that day at lunchtime, I should have known she wasn't going to skirt the surface for long. I was on a break from classes at Purdue. At over eighty, her voice was shaky, but that day it also had edge. She rushed the small talk. Then Mary Ruth zeroed in.

"When are you going to join the Campus Crusade for Christ?"

Halfway through my sandwich, I stopped chewing. Every so often I could hear the oxygen shoot from her tank in spurts. *Sst-sst.*

Sst-sst. I managed to swallow my bite, although it seemed to have ballooned to three times its size.

What did she know? I wondered. Who had told her?

A month earlier I had written a letter to my extended family announcing my impending conversion. Not so much detailing why, just explaining that I was no longer accepting Christmas gifts, and that I was trying to maintain a basic kosher diet (no pork or shellfish). I'd also talked about how this was a natural decision for me to make, but in closing I'd added a brief request that no one communicate my decision to my grandparents, Harry and Mary Ruth, the people who had sent me countless Christian-themed birthday cards and paid my way to every Vacation Bible School. They were heading toward ninety, both with their own long lists of health concerns. Wouldn't knowledge of my conversion just cause undue stress? At worst, in the few years they had left, it would instigate a rift between us.

Otherwise my letter was celebratory, because to become Jewish is no simple endeavor. Of conversion, Rabbi Tvzi Freeman writes, "[B]ecoming Jewish is very much like becoming an American. . . . You can't come to a country and declare yourself a member. It's a two-way street: aside from you choosing your country, the government of that country has to decide to accept you. Similarly, if you choose Judaism, you also need Judaism to choose you." For me this involved reading book after book, attending Shabbat and High Holy services, engaging with a sponsoring rabbi, and acquiring an understanding of Jewish history and culture, all of which took a long time.

That passage took almost half a decade, though much of what happened at first was internal exploration, followed by dabbling, then a formal process that lasted around two years. More than anything, converting took integrating myself into a community that had a tendency to eye interested outsiders with a type of practical suspicion. A community that expected any newcomer wouldn't, upon learning the conversion requirements, stick around, because most didn't.

There's angst among practicing Jews over dwindling numbers, and no doubt some of this is tied to the endurance test of Jewish conversion. It takes seconds to declare oneself a Christian but years to become Jewish, and I wonder how that's affected the numbers of each group. How would Christianity change if each new follower was required to complete a high level of spiritual inquiry and scholarship? How would Judaism transform if outsiders could simply recite a prayer, make a spiritual commitment, and be welcomed into the community? So much of converting to Judaism is a study in patience, like knocking over and over at the same door.

For some it opens. For me it did. But here was my grandmother reminding me of what I already knew about Christianity: its unsettling tendency to do the opposite, to pound at the door of any soul searching for answers.

Panic of my grandmother knowing about my conversion beat through me. Mentally I fumbled through nieces and nephews, aunts and uncles, attempting to figure out who had spilled the beans, but by then her question had hung on the line long enough.

"I'm still thinking of joining the Crusade," I heard myself say.

"Good," Mary Ruth said. Her oxygen tank hissed. "That's my girl."

Our conversation meandered to a few other topics, but I got off the phone as quickly as possible. Enraged, exasperated, that afternoon I resolved to distance myself from my Southern Baptist namesake. I had lied. I had failed to tell my evangelizing eighty-six-year-old grandmother about my imminent breach with Christianity, so in the following weeks and months I proceeded down the easiest path: avoidance. I ignored her. Calls, letters unanswered. I wouldn't visit either, and in this way the secret itself instigated the very rift I had tried to sidestep.

What surprised me, as that rift deepened in the years that followed, was how much I began to miss Mary Ruth. Sometimes I found myself recalling the moments we had shared together, bouts of brutal honesty and all.

The summer after my high school graduation my grandmother bought us cruise tickets on a Carnival Fun Ship headed for Jamaica. It was a gift so lavish I couldn't decline. We boarded the ship at Galveston on a cloudless, hot, and humid Texas day.

Little did I know that our trip included an itinerary—not Carnival Fun Ship's, but Mary Ruth's—of waking at 6 each morning for an hour of prayer and guided Bible study. My grandmother provided me with a book by Rick Warren called *A Purpose Driven Life* which, like most other Christian texts, I couldn't quite relate to. In our small room with an ocean view, during this early hour at sea, I would dream of throwing myself overboard. Occasionally I could hear couples bumping past our door, still drunk from the night before, laughing, rummaging for their keys and shouting, *Shit!*

But other than reading the gospels, we had a decent time together. In Jamaica my grandmother bought me a red sarong that lifted with the breeze and we marveled at the water. Other than that one subject of religion, we had always enjoyed one another's company, I realized. Like the days as a young girl when I would visit her in Hot Springs, Arkansas, where my grandparents eventually retired, and she would drive me to the local rock shop and let me select a few semi-precious stones to keep (or lose, as I often did): jasper, tiger's-eye, turquoise. At each breakfast she'd make me finish my milk before leaving the table, but if I refused, she'd let me stir in chocolate syrup. On our best days together, Mary Ruth took me to the natatorium with her to swim, where from the shallow end I'd watch her do laps, her arms coming up and over the water, strong and repeating, her height noticeable even beneath the surface.

This I still wonder: how much distance would Mary Ruth have put between us, knowing I had chosen Judaism? Did she already know? Is that why she called that day, agitated, rushed?

How much distance did I put between us by not telling her?

☾

MARY RUTH DIED three days before her ninetieth birthday and by then I couldn't remember our last interaction. Even worse, afterward, a memory of my grandmother crept up and would not let me go. It implied I had made a serious mistake in not telling her, and in the weeks after her death I replayed that memory, each time becoming more convinced I had underestimated Mary Ruth's ability to love—despite, in her view, the ultimate disagreement.

When I was twelve my parents enrolled me in confirmation classes at Wildwood United Methodist Church. It was our family's longtime church in Houston and my sister Lauren and I took the class with about ten other preteens. We met each Wednesday night after school and at the end of the five-week course the plan was to have us baptized in front of the congregation.

The class was taught by Wildwood Methodist's new pastor, Reverend Ron Findley, a man who had previously made a living selling cars. Middle-aged and overconfident, the reverend had a warm demeanor that was either highly practiced or innate, one could never be sure.

On that first Wednesday night pizza was delivered and we gathered in a brightly lit Sunday school classroom. Once we had served ourselves and taken seats, Reverend Findley sauntered up to the whiteboard, a slice with pepperoni in hand. He wrote JEWS on one side and CHRISTIANS on the other. Jews, he said, taking a big bite, were fundamentally different than Christians. Even though Christians shared a history with the Jewish people, we were not to think of them as the same as us.

"It's all about the way we see God," he said, swallowing. "Genesis 32: Jacob wrestles all night with an angel. All night, my friends. At dawn he is given a new name. He is given the name Israel, which to this day is the name of the Jews. And let's be crystal clear about that translation." The reverend paused, letting his gaze sweep the room. "Israel means to struggle with God."

Reverend Findley took another bite of pizza, chewed, and swallowed. He set the slice down and wiped his mouth with a napkin. Then he picked up his Bible and held it high in the air. "But here's the good news, my friends. We Christians have Jesus, and Jesus was perfect."

Reverend Findley invited us to open our Bibles to the same verse and the room filled with the sound of people thumbing through pages, but I kept staring at the board.

No one had put it quite like that before. Israel means to struggle with God. For as long as I could remember, it had been a struggle. Not so much with God, but with Jesus. I desperately wanted to believe in everything Christianity had to offer—perfect man, ultimate sacrifice—and I longed to embody the servant-like nature of those surrounding me at church, old and young, all bowed heads and open hearts.

Strangely, though, it was this deep desire to fit into my congregation, and my family, that kept striking me as false. It was what I wanted, but it was not who I was. The greater part of me that didn't believe in Jesus's divinity was gentler. Strong, abiding, steady, as if waiting for the right time to speak up.

At twelve years old the implications of not believing still terrified me—not believing meant burning, which I hated to think about—though whatever was holding me back from accepting that belief did not feel threatening. It held me in kindness mostly, but at other moments in an embrace that was more challenging, like the way boxers cling to one another between blows.

Try as I had throughout the years, I was never able to reconcile the idea of Christ, of pure perfection in human form, with what seemed to me a universal and simple truth. Humans were most beautiful and holy *with* their jagged edges and soft spots, not devoid of them. Not scrubbed clean and propped up on a platform, but tinted with frustration and failures, chances to change and grow. It wasn't that I didn't believe Jesus existed, but that I believed in a different Jesus: Jesus the carpenter, the upstart seeking to reform his own religion, a man who eventually died for his cause, a human being who was deeply flawed but kept fighting. Someone who wrestled with God until the end, and who, dying, called out: My father, my father, why have you forsaken me?

Jesus the Jew.

Jesus, I thought again, a Jew.

Nothing more, nothing less.

My eyes shot around the Sunday school classroom. Was anyone else making this connection? Even if my realization had been delivered by, of all people, Reverend Ron Findley, it explained everything. It meant everything. A sudden clarity inundated the room. The part of me that had been waiting to speak up was, for the first time, speaking. Speaking everywhere: inside me, in the Sunday school room, down the hall, and for all I knew in the pines outside the church and in my family's house down the road.

Stunned, I looked around.

Five weeks later after the last class, Reverend Findley lined us up outside his office. He called each student in one by one to ask a series of questions. He had given us the most important question beforehand, so it was like a test I knew I was going to bomb before it even started.

Had I opened my heart to Jesus?

In a way, yes, but it wasn't the Jesus Christianity presented. Sixth or seventh in line, I watched as those in front me left the office, their faces beaming in a mix of relief and pride. Some wore a newfound righteousness. My sister was one of them, a Mona Lisa smirk on her face as she breezed down the hallway toward the parking lot. I watched her open the door and step out into the sunlight. I shifted, waiting for my turn.

In the office, Reverend Findley greeted me with his invincible grin and invited me to sit down. "Have you opened your heart to Jesus?"

I stared at him. How could I begin to explain what had happened to me? That I didn't see Christianity as wrong, only different, that it was like a song that moved some but not others, and never in me. I'm sorry, I wanted to say, but not to him. Those were words for my family.

"I have doubts," I mumbled.

A stir of disappointment flickered across Reverend Findley's face, but his smile held. He leaned back in his chair. "You know, Natalie, the teen years can be very tricky." His smile broadened. "Let's see what we can do about these doubts."

"No." I stood and left.

☾

THE FOLLOWING SUNDAY the church was a full house. Relatives had traveled to witness their loved ones get baptized, and as they considered it a life-altering event well worth a visit, my grandmother and grandpa had flown from Hot Springs to see Lauren get confirmed. Mary Ruth was dressed to the nines that morning in a conservative pink skirt she had tailored herself. She was radiant and chatty with the members of Wildwood Methodist, though I noticed she was avoiding me.

Right before the beginning of the service Reverend Findley rounded up all the members of the confirmation class, steering us to the front row of the church. Services began. After an opening hymn Reverend Findley welcomed the large crowd before him, then he motioned to us, calling "all those being baptized to join him up on stage."

This was when I discovered that I was the only one who had decided not to be baptized.

My decision left me sitting at the front row of the church alone. As I watched my classmates file up to the front, a chill swept up my neck. Suddenly I could feel the entire congregation at my back. My heartbeat thrummed in my ears and my face grew hot, and all at once I was ashamed of the honest choice I had made.

It takes a long time to baptize a dozen people, I learned that morning, and Reverend Findley made it seem like an eternity. In my row I focused on not reacting. Not crying. Trying to look as if nothing was wrong, studying the same patch of red carpet for so long I started to believe I could fall into it and disappear. I managed to lift my face when Reverend Findley called Lauren's name. As I watched my sister get baptized I felt sick, at once too far away and much too close to the scene unfolding around me. Then I felt like exploding.

Then I heard something coming from behind me: the sound of footsteps. I turned to see Mary Ruth approaching. She had left her seat many rows back and, striding to the front of Wildwood Methodist, pink skirt swishing, tall as ever, my grandmother glided down the front row to sit beside me. I knew she had prayed I would be up there with my older sister, and so this is still what haunts me, the memory of that moment, the way she put her arm around me.

I leaned into her warmth, breathed her in, and my heartbeat decelerated into a discernable rhythm. Even at twelve, I knew that what my grandmother did that morning came straight from the heart of Christianity. Not the preaching or proselytizing, not the saving of lost souls, but something more straightforward. It was the simple instinct to go to someone vulnerable, alone, the glaring misfit in a crowd, and to sit with them. That day if I was the leper, Mary Ruth was Jesus.

Christianity, I realized then, was letting me go.

I closed my eyes and thanked God for my grandmother.

I went home and wept.

4

SLOW LIFE

THERE IS ONLY so much furniture one can move before the wrists give out. Couches, hutches, boxes of books, the dining room table carefully hauled through the front door. At our first dinner in the big white farmhouse holding my fork involved a conscious effort. My wrists were worn out. Should've ordered takeout, I thought, realizing then that would have meant a drive into Ludington, fifteen miles away. On our first night in the Michigan countryside, that's what I was thinking about: the bother of driving, wasted gas, the art of doing without.

To say it was about the gas, however, is only half accurate. Closer to the full truth is that there were a multitude of firsts that went into moving into that house, and being a novice, I somehow banked on having the energy to do it all on day one. Maybe most first-time homeowners make this mistake—underestimating the time and energy it takes to make a new space one's own, filling it with objects belonging to some former residence, some former life. Moving wears a person down in strange places, the wrists, the elbows, the calves, and it left me bruised at the shins. Sleep proved restless until everything was in its right nook. And where was that nook, I kept wondering, unboxing my things, in this new and old house?

It took us five days to move in completely. On the sixth, we walked next door. Next door was a quarter mile down the road, but we wanted to introduce ourselves to the older couple who lived in the attractive yellow home north of us.

"These people can't be our neighbors," I told Joe on the walk over. "They live so far away. We can't see them. They can't see us." I pointed to a stand of spruces. "Look. There's an entire stretch of woods between our houses."

"Out here they are neighbors," Joe countered. As usual his stride was at a tempo that matched my own. It was something I had always appreciated, that we walked at a similar pace. "And aren't the best neighbors the ones you can't see?"

"Sure. Like the kind who don't hear a peep if you're hollering for help in the middle of the night."

In a way, we had already met the older couple next door. One morning, driving a truckload past their house, we had spotted them outside weeding their irises. They paused and looked up. They waved. We waved back. That May, like every May since, their yard was resplendent: weeping cherry trees and mulched gardens, large pink stones and a tulip-lined drive. It gave the place a sense of warmth and cleanliness, and I wondered what they made of Replica Dodge, or of us, the young people who had bought Bill's property. I imagined how grateful they were for that quarter-mile stretch of woods that separated the two properties.

On the porch Joe knocked on the door and a man of about seventy-five opened up. He was in excellent shape. "James Skipton," he said, extending his hand. "You must be the new neighbors." James invited us to sit and we settled into a set of white wicker chairs on the front porch.

As soon as he started talking I noticed James didn't subscribe to the stall-speak I had come to expect from Michiganders. The way they tended to say something and then wait, taking stock of everyone's reactions, before saying anything else. James had little to no verbal tiptoe, and I liked him instantly for it. During that visit he talked almost nonstop, proving himself knowledgeable about the area, our four acres, and his own thirty-six that surrounded Replica Dodge. It was through this initial conversation we discovered that he and his wife, Helen, who by then had joined us on the porch, had owned the big white farmhouse before Bill.

"So you lived at Replica Dodge before it was Replica Dodge?" I asked, almost cutting him off.

"Yes," James answered. He pursed his lips.

I could tell he was thinking of saying something else, but didn't. Instead he went on about the history of the house, how it was built in 1896, how almost a century later he and his wife had raised their two daughters, Beth and Nora, in that home. He paused to take a drink of water. "That house raises good girls."

Helen had tanned skin that revealed stark white lines on her neck whenever she turned her handsome face toward the road. It was apparent she had been on the listening end of James's talk for years. She said very little during our first visit, although she seemed to enjoy her husband's banter. Or at least she wore a satisfied smile, as if she knew there were two types of talkers in this world, the ones who had interesting things to say, and the ones who simply prattled on. Helen had ended up with the former.

"If you meet anyone over sixty," James said a half hour later, "tell them you live in the George Awl place. Owned most of this land, up and down and beyond. Bought it from a tribe in the late 1800s, built that house, all three thousand feet of it." James took off his sun hat. "There's been little change in the floor plan since the house went up, though when we had it we dug out the basement—if you consider that an addition—and we found a remarkable cistern. Tried to leave it intact, but the construction workers just kept running into problems. In any case that basement stays very cool, even on the hottest days of August."

As James continued to talk, I tried to imagine our property as the Skiptons had it, before Replica Dodge was built. Replica Dodge minus Replica Dodge. It was difficult. It was so difficult I couldn't do it, so instead I tried to picture George Awl, original owner, but all I came up with was an approximation of the Monopoly man. Sometime thereafter the conversation came to a natural close and we stood to leave.

"So glad two young people finally bought that place," James said. He shook our hands and we turned back toward the road. He beamed in the evening light. "Nobody else can do that much work."

☾

Sitting on the farmhouse porch I could hear vehicles coming up and over the hills.

That was the quiet, I soon learned, of Replica Dodge. One could listen to that slow whir of tires on gravel, a low gear shifting to high—the sound of a single truck coming—for miles. At last the vehicle would slide into view, pass our house, and disappear again down the road into the hardwoods. Across it the cherry trees stood like soldiers in formation. Someone had mentioned that freak warm temperatures in March meant those trees wouldn't fruit in July.

Some afternoons it seemed that no one drove by, and on those afternoons the road ceased being a road and returned to a feral passage for deer, rabbits, a litter of coyote pups led by their watchful mother. I wish I could say it was all bucolically appealing, but instead, after the moving frenzy, the rural slowness coiled up something in me so tight I could hardly stand it.

I knew there was work to be done but I couldn't see what needed attention. I didn't know enough about country life to begin to understand what James Skipton meant by "that much work," so instead I found myself wallowing in intense observation.

I stared at the becalmed little city from our porch. A buzzard circled the extra acreage and landed on the roof of the Lady's Emporium. It was as if I'd taken a leap back in time to Dodge City's heyday, early 1900s, only I was stuck on some two-bit ghost ranch on the far outskirts of town. I thought of camping in Texas as a girl, of the long drive from Houston my family would make each summer to Double Lake, exchanging air-conditioning for briars, bugs, and birdsong, wet bark and honeysuckle. The deprivation of all those usual creature comforts generated an emptiness inside that both freed and terrified me.

I roamed the property hunting for cell phone reception. I went around in circles until I finally hit on a limited radius in the yard where my phone got a few bars, the single spot where I could stand, stock-still, to talk with family and friends. *How are you settling in?* they wondered. *Are you lonely yet?* they asked. What they really wanted to know: *Is the city girl in you dissolving? Thinning out like paint cut with water?*

I had to make sure not to move beyond the black walnut tree, where I would lose them.

From that same spot in the yard Joe and I later phoned local internet providers who cursorily informed us we lived outside their service area. How stupid of me, I thought then, assuming the internet would be up and running. How stupid, out here in Replica Dodge, to expect I'd remain a member of the digital age.

In an era of smartphones and tablets, of being a click away from news, social media, and goods, Replica Dodge had cut me off. Suddenly lofty spiritual fears of being isolated from other Jews were replaced by far more practical problems. What about my family? Friends? Emails for work? Time retreated even further from the meandering pace we'd known in Ludington as the gait of small-town life along Lake Michigan. Now with no tourists, no town, little to no cell reception, and no digital age, our days seemed to sputter out into nothingness.

At worst, I kept telling myself, we would get a landline. But three weeks after moving in, the only option for internet service we'd found was a satellite operation.

"Too expensive," Joe said. "And at best service will be spotty." It was morning. We were standing in the kitchen, waiting for our eggs to fry in the pan.

"I don't care, let's get it." I put two slices of bread in the toaster. "I don't even know what's happening in the world."

"Do you need it?" Joe shrugged, leaning back. "Does it mean that much to you?"

I spun around to face him. "Which one, Joe? The internet? Or the world?"

☾

AS MY INSIDES coiled tight, I saw enough to know that we had entered what was, what had always been, a natural habitat for Joe: the Michigan countryside.

Despite his mildness, despite starting this search on my terms, I couldn't help but notice we had ended up right where he wanted to be. Slow life became my future husband. There was no growing into Replica Dodge for Joe. He was already home.

Worse, I knew that I had gravitated toward Replica Dodge just as much as, maybe even more than, Joe. The strange town, the big white farmhouse, the barn, the extra two acres wild with autumn olive. For almost a year I had refused every place in Ludington, houses nicer than the one we owned now. And this I also knew: had I said no to any of it—moving to Michigan after college, the decision to purchase this place—Joe would have yielded.

But I was adrift. The sluggishness of years spent in the country stretched in front of me, miles away from any type of Jewish community and further still from my birthplace. As I watched Joe explore the property with a giddy, exuberant energy I'd rarely seen him exhibit before, one thing became clear. Joe was happy. And I was on the porch.

Had he even noticed?

Before moving to Mason County, the fact that Joe wasn't Jewish had always struck me as a small misfortune in an otherwise ideal mate. No one's a perfect fit, and so what if we believed differently? Who knew, maybe that was even for the best. We had met well before my conversion and Joe had been supportive throughout it, though always from the distance of someone who could never quite make sense of organized religion.

Raised Catholic, Joe had a soft spot for what he called religion's "optimal functions." These optimal functions included an emphasis on humility and service to others, and the idea of examining one's attitudes in order to develop a strong moral compass. But doctrine was another matter, and I knew better than to press anyone on issues of belief. My conversion had been a personal decision, and Joe's distance from religion wasn't judgmental. He had none of the gloating acrimony I'd witnessed in other science-minded people when they spoke of religion, though science seemed as close to a guiding spiritual philosophy as I could identify in Joe.

Until now, that had been fine. Until Mason County, I had always assumed I could have them both: a Jewish community and Joe. Even if my future husband wasn't Jewish, there would be services to attend, Shabbat Seders to enjoy with friends, High Holy Day celebrations and observances, with or without him by my side. Good enough.

But now the nearest temple was almost a hundred miles away. I had made my choice, banking that someday things would be different, that we would leave and start somewhere new eventually, but it didn't help that as I struggled to adjust, Joe seemed to float. He was fluent in rural life like it was his first language. He pruned the grapes with tools I didn't know he had. He waved at the mailman each day at 4, then whistled on his way to get the mail.

This *is* a first language for him, I reminded myself. Joe had grown up in Alpena, Michigan, an area exceedingly similar to Mason County, only on the east side of the state. It was rural, blue collar, and nestled along one of the Great Lakes (Huron), and though the differences between his childhood home and Mason County seemed numerous to him, to me the two places shared a striking resemblance.

I watched him taking samples of earth, trying to pinpoint the best spot in Replica Dodge to start a garden. Somehow, shortly after launching into full-blown adulthood, Joe had already secured much of what he wanted in life: a great job, a house in the Michigan countryside, and a dark-haired woman who was smart and driven (and willing to risk being miles away from the Jews she had just joined). *Joe sheen.* That's what his few friends had called it years ago, right after he'd spiked the volleyball over the net to win a game.

"Joe sheen?"

"You haven't seen it? The boy's got something."

Yeah? I'd thought at the time. So do I.

One morning Joe came into the bathroom as I was toweling off my hair. "There's a bird caught in one of the barn's pillars. I need your help."

As soon as I opened the front door I heard it. The squawking: high-pitched and demented, the unmistakable shrieking of a creature moments before its death from exhaustion. The bird's wings beat against the inside of the pillar.

Joe was running an extension cord from the barn. At the pillar he plugged in his drill. I stood a good distance away.

"What do you want me to do?"

"In a moment, I'm going to open this pillar. I need you to watch and make sure the bird gets somewhere safe."

"Somewhere safe?"

"A tree or a post. Anywhere but the ground."

"Alright."

Suddenly the bird was quiet.

"Is it dead?"

Joe didn't answer. He worked quickly. The bird's wings started up again more furiously than ever. It was now focusing all its energy on getting out. Joe leaned his shoulder against the piece of wood and removed the final screw. "One." He sucked in a breath. "Two." He ducked. "Three."

Joe wrenched the wood back and the bird—a robin—tore out of the darkness. It landed on a nearby spruce, its stark orange chest heaving. It drank the open air like water.

"Safe," I said.

Joe exhaled and grinned.

Goddammit, I thought. There *is* something about him.

That's what was tough about having said yes to Joe's proposal. For the first time, here in Replica Dodge, I was no longer on an equal footing with him. It was as if I was running as hard as I could, knowing that I was just as fast as Joe, just as smart, just as hardworking—but somehow, none of my efforts had yet met with success. I was trying to adjust to Mason County but failing, just as I had interviewed for jobs but secured no offers. The competitive drive that had once pushed us together was pushing us apart.

We are not simply a team, I wanted to say. *We are a match.* Yet for better or worse it was terrifying to think I had fallen behind at the exact wrong moment, now that the stakes were high, now that we were no longer college students artfully debating over the phone, but adults beginning a life together.

I watched the robin for a few minutes before heading back to the porch. I twisted my engagement ring around my finger, then took it off. Already there was a pale line where the ring had blocked the sun. I put it in the center of my palm. For something so small, it carried a surprising amount of weight. Eventually, I told myself for the hundredth time, I would find my way back to a Jewish community.

Unfortunately for my future husband, already at home in these rolling Mason County acres, already saving robins trapped in barn pillars, Jews didn't tend to live in the country. A Jew in the country. What a strange notion. What a non sequitur, I thought, remembering that term I had learned as a girl from my father, the philosophy professor. I stared at the ring in my palm. Non sequitur: an unnamed fallacy that invalidates the entire argument. "Non sequitur," I said out loud, Latin for *It does not follow*.

5

WELCOME TO ALPENA

THERE WAS NO preamble to our first kiss. Almost a decade before Joe and I had been friends for some time, but I had hesitated to take things further. It wasn't as if I didn't think of him in that way. Joe was smart, kind, and he made me laugh. And unlike most of the attractive men I'd met in Houston, despite his good looks, Joe showed no interest in making them a cornerstone of his person.

When I was an English major at the University of Houston, Joe would call me from Michigan Tech and say things that launched me so far outside myself I couldn't help but clutch the phone a little tighter. This is what made Joe stand out it my mind, and linger. Mostly they were thoughts that had nothing to do with me, or the human race, or even Earth, like how no one knew for sure what shape our universe was in, or how far it stretched, or if it would start collapsing in on itself at some unknown future date.

I want to be with those who know secret things, the poet Rainer Maria Rilke wrote, *or else alone.*

As far as I could tell, Joe, an enthusiastic physics major, knew secret things. Thrilling things. Things my writer friends, literature professors, and humanities-inclined family could never even touch. *Look inside*, these people seemed to say, gesturing always to accentuate the self. *There you'll find your answer.*

No, Joe would counter. *The answers are out there.*

Despite all this pale-blue-dot thinking, Joe had taken a persistent personal interest in me. He was a heliocentric person who thought of human beings as small players in a far more complex and exquisite equation, yet oddly enough, I somehow existed as the exception to that rule. I liked how I could draw out the most human part of Joe, a bright mind that was otherwise preoccupied with patterns and formulas.

From the start of our friendship he was patient but purposeful. As a junior at Michigan Tech, he bought phone cards to call me each week and he would write too, emails that stayed mostly platonic until they veered, depending on the time of day, sometimes late at night, into something else entirely.

In those early conversations I challenged almost everything Joe said. I was good at debating because my father had taught philosophy for twenty years and I knew how to express, support, and steer arguments forward. We debated about the Peace Corps, the existence of God, how famous poets and scientists often made deplorable human beings. An air of charged competition grew up between us, and we became good at disagreeing, adept at identifying and acknowledging the shakier ground of our own arguments as well as each other's. Science versus art. Southern hospitality versus midwestern modesty. City living versus country life.

I liked Joe, but he lived in another state, and I stayed busy in Texas. The only time I saw him was when I flew to Michigan, on break from my classes, to my family's new house in a state I barely knew existed before my freshman year in college, when my father took a promotion and my family left Houston for good.

☾

AFTER GRADUATING FROM high school I went to the closest university that had accepted me, right downtown. Self-centered, brooding, and beginning to be called Ruth, I attacked my classes with the motivation of someone who desperately needed to prove her maturity for college-level courses, and I failed to notice that on weekends back home, in the suburbs, my parents spoke increasingly of new opportunities. They had grown weary of Houston traffic, the endless construction, and the light pollution that made the stars hard to see, even on a clear night.

A little way through my freshman year, my parents announced they would be relocating to Alpena, Michigan. We were in the middle of dinner. I shot a look at Lauren, not sure of what to make of the announcement. She was trying not to laugh.

"Where is that?" I asked.

"Nowhere," my sister answered.

A week later a promotional DVD arrived in our mailbox courtesy of Alpena, Michigan. I watched it with Lauren the next weekend I was home. It went something like this:

Ah, the sunrise!
Lake Huron's rocky shore!
Big guys hoisting speckled fish!
Old people with wind in their hair!
Little kids frolicking in the fountain!
A bizarre deficiency of black people!
Beer tents!

I laughed so hard I fell off the couch. "This is where people go to die," I said. "Like dogs under the porch."

☾

MY FATHER HAD accepted a presidency position at the community college of Alpena, much like the one in Mason County where Joe and I would eventually land. Both institutions were counted in the "small ten": community colleges that served mostly rural populations and were often the only higher education option for entire regions of the state. The college wanted my father to begin as soon as possible, which meant that my mother, sister, and I were left to pack up our house in Lexington Woods. I would stay behind at the University of Houston; everyone else would move. My father flew to Michigan the day after Christmas.

Having lived in the Lexington Woods house all my life, as we began to pack, I felt the need to snap mental portraits of every room, nook, and cranny of our modest one-story. My parents had gotten married in the living room. That year my mother had planted a sycamore that had since grown to shade the window of my bedroom, even in the worst Texas heat. In the kitchen, in removing a framed Rothko print, Lauren and I rediscovered the dark lines from when my father had settled into a book, forgotten about the beans he had put in the pressure cooker, and they had exploded, rocketing out to paint black streaks across the walls.

As the packing wore on, the jokes about Alpena wore out. The further into the moving process we got, the less amusing everything became. My father was gone. My mother was exasperated with the task at hand. Here was the house they had brought each of us home to as newborns, and here were its contents, drained out as if in some peculiar embalming process, rearranged to fit into the back of a single moving truck. By the final day of packing, there was nothing funny about Alpena, Michigan.

Positive my parents had traded Houston for a box of rocks, on the following spring break, I took my first plane from Houston to Detroit. Then another, smaller one, what someone next to me called a *puddle jumper*, further north. The puddle jumper was loud and cramped, and an hour later, I panicked when, glancing out the window, it seemed as if we were descending into an abandoned field.

What the hell was happening? Why wasn't the captain telling us what had gone wrong? At eighteen all I had known of airports involved dozens of terminals, magazine and smoothie stands, honking cabs, seven-level parking garages, and conveyor belts delivering one piece of black luggage after the next.

The plane bumped down on a plowed strip of pavement outside a single-roomed building. "Welcome to Alpena!" the pilot declared.

☾

IN THAT MOMENT, even before disembarking, I thought I'd hate everything about Michigan. The state, the people in it, even my parents for leaving me behind after I had selected a college so close to home. In a fit of despair rife with teenage melodrama, I spent the following days adamant in my resolve to be repulsed at every aspect of my parents' new life. Lauren did her best to cheer me up, acknowledging how different Alpena was from Houston while trying to highlight some of the small town's features: the Huron lakefront, the picturesque main street with its host of coffee shops, shoe stores, bars and restaurants. We could walk to anything as long as we were bundled up.

"There's a guy on campus I want you to meet," she mentioned. "He seems perfect for you."

Lauren was always trying to set me up. "Not interested."

"If we see him I'll point him out. I've asked around. He has a good reputation. That's one benefit of a town like this. It's hard to hide a bad history here. Everyone knows everyone and everyone knows everything. It's very strange. Anyways, he's kind of a loner, but plays soccer. Super hot. Stands out in this town because he has dreadlocks down his back."

"He's black? Where did you find a black person up here? I haven't seen anything but white faces since the plane left Detroit."

She rolled her eyes. "He's one of those weirdo white guys with dreads. Now get dressed. Let me show you around."

That day Lauren brought her friend Katie along to the college, where I found my father hunched over his new computer in a corner office three times the size of the one he'd had in Houston. Months into his new job, it still looked as if he had just moved in. This confused me. His office was neat but almost empty, yet none of his stuff was missing. My mom had brought it all. Everything he owned filled only a quarter of this new office.

As he guided me into the main office to introduce me to his staff, even as they said things like *We're so excited your father's here as president,* his title seemed foreign, as if there had been some mix-up, one that had landed my dad, a liberal philosophy professor from Houston, in the wrong building, the wrong job, in the wrong state.

Later, when we entered the library, Lauren turned to face me. "There he is," she said.

"Who?" asked Katie.

"The guy I want her to meet." Lauren pointed to the back of the room where a series of tables were set up for study groups, several occupied by students poring over magazines, chatting with each other, some still wearing the winter coats that seemed to eat them alive. At the middle table sat Joe. Alone. Textbook open, pencil in hand.

"You mean Joe?" Katie said. "Everyone has a crush on Joe."

"There's no point," I began, but Lauren was halfway across the room, squirreling over to him.

Then Joe was in front us. He looked puzzled but shook my hand. I took him in. He was tall, lean, olive-skinned. He had green eyes that bordered on blue and his dark lashes were so long that at first I thought they were fake.

"This is my sister Natalie," Lauren said, forgetting, as she had all morning, to introduce me as Ruth. From then on Joe would call me Natalie, a fact that took on a life of its own as increasingly, people from Houston—friends, professors—called me Ruth, yet everyone in Michigan knew me as Natalie. After years of flying between the two locations, it was as if each name had a distinct identity tied to its ensuing destination. Flying home to Houston as Ruth the writer, touching down in Alpena as Natalie, daughter, sister, new girl in town.

After a lengthy silence in which Lauren kept staring at me like *What is your problem? He's standing right here!* I pointed to his sweatshirt. "You like Less Than Jake?"

He nodded. "You like them?"

"I've met them."

Another pause opened up between us and Katie filled it. She filled it with stories, with anecdotes of growing up in the countryside down the road from Joe. He had worn his hair long since childhood, kept growing it even when people regularly mistook him for a girl.

"Long hair is about as low maintenance as you get," Joe finally added five minutes later. "You set dreadlocks and you don't have to pay a barber or brush your hair. I got to get to class."

Lauren insisted we meet again. She offered to invite Joe to my birthday party. Lauren had lived in Alpena for less than three months, in the dreariest part of the year in Michigan, but somehow my sister had met enough people to fill the indoor pool of my family's new residence on Washington Avenue. She wanted to celebrate before I left for Houston, before we wouldn't see each other again until the next June, and I acquiesced.

"We can party, but I wouldn't bother inviting him. He's probably completely flavorless, like this town."

Invited or not, Joe didn't come.

Over the coming months, however, something happened. Back in Houston I became more confident on my own, and maybe this is what made my attitude toward Alpena soften at the edges: that even as I grew more confident, I still missed my family so much that I began looking forward to those puddle-jumper trips. Taking the puddle jumper out of Detroit meant being close to my mother, my father, and my sister again.

Almost a year later, the following December, Joe approached me at an Alpena Community College basketball game I attended with my dad. I was surprised by how glad I was to see him again. His canvas pants and beautiful face, his snow boots on the verge of holes. He invited me to go midnight sledding with him. So, I thought, not completely flavorless: nobody had ever invited me sledding before, let alone at midnight.

Joe told me to meet him at a place called Cramer's Truck Stop and I tried to mask my cringe. A truck stop seemed an odd place to meet for a first date, but Joe didn't seem to register this. Either he didn't know about the unspoken norms of the dating world or he didn't care about them, but either way I was curious.

Cramer's was closed when I arrived, and I stood in the freezing dark. I began to consider how little I knew about Joe, this person I was meeting alone. I looked ridiculous in the giant yellow snowsuit I had pulled over my clothes. But then Joe was there, pulling up in a beat-up Buick Regal. He leaned over and swung the door open. In the glow of the car's overhead light, he grinned. "Hey." His teeth were crooked and jammed together, but he was striking.

We drove to a hill far outside of town. We parked and Joe turned the car lights on to illuminate the high-sloped snow. Then we hiked up. At the top of Manning Hill, Joe showed me how to give a running start before jumping on the sled, and I managed to tuck myself in just before it careened downward.

When I think about that night now, I remember the speed of the sled. It was incredibly fast. It felt dangerous whipping in and out of the car's lights with the dark trees on either side of us. I remember the fresh snow churning up in my face as we hurtled downhill. It was freezing, but after hiking up the hill a second time, I started to sweat under my snowsuit. I wriggled out of it, getting down to my jeans and sweater, as Joe retrieved a second sled. I remember we didn't talk much, but when we did, I was at the top of the hill and Joe was at the bottom, and we were hollering over the wind and trees in this empty, sublime place that swallowed one's voice and returned nothing but more dark and cold.

The dates I went on in Houston with guys from the city—poetry readings, patio dining, tango lessons—suddenly seemed dwarfed by these Michigan excursions with Joe. From then on, most of the things we found to do were free or low cost, and usually involved being out in nature. A walk to the local dam or duck sanctuary, maybe, or just hanging out at one of our houses. During the summer months there was volleyball at the beach with his small circle of friends.

Falling asleep one night with liquor in my veins, sand in my swimsuit, I finally admitted to myself there could, just possibly, be something to glean from the tiny town of Alpena. It wasn't Houston. It wasn't home. But at the very least, there was Joe the physics major.

As the youngest of five children born into a Catholic family, Joe had spent his childhood among horses, turkeys, and dogs with fur like wild boar. His father was in building maintenance, his mother a part-time caretaker for the disabled. He still lived with his parents on some cedar-rich acreage just outside Alpena, in the small house his father and uncles had built with their own hands. After graduating from high school he had done his first two years at the local community college, eventually transferring to Michigan Tech.

This history produced a blend of hardscrabble values in Joe that seemed to alternately deride and scaffold the future he was, even then, scrambling toward: one in higher education. Something strong in him also struggled against the academic life, the one I had always known as the daughter of a professor. Years later, after he'd secured his tenure-track position, I noticed that whenever anyone asked Joe what he did for a living, he would respond flatly, "I teach" rather than "I'm a professor." "Everyone hates professors," he explained to me, winking.

☾

Joe's blue-collar pride resurfaced when we were packing our things to move to Replica Dodge, as I started to grasp the extent to which he was reluctant to throw anything out. A few days into packing, I realized he was clinging most to things that reminded him of his childhood in Alpena. Thin hand-sewn pillowcases, deeply stained but unchipped coffee mugs, and he insisted on continuing to drive the truck his father had given him. Each morning he parked the old Dodge alongside a host of faculty-owned newer Toyota Priuses and Subarus, where it stood out, green and rusty, like a bruise.

"Don't you want a new truck?" I kept asking.

"Runs fine," he would say.

The night we went sledding Joe became my first friend in Michigan. He called me when I went back to Texas and wrote often, and maybe this was the preamble to our first kiss. If so I missed it, or more likely willfully ignored it. I didn't like that I was beginning to feel for someone from the state that had uprooted my parents—and with it, my own life—so in the following months I tried not to notice as Joe and I became increasingly attached, as those occasional flirtations in his emails became abiding questions that I was also asking myself. Was a long-distance relationship workable? Was it worth it? We continued our phone debates and on breaks between semesters, we saw each other as much as possible.

One afternoon, back in Alpena for Christmas, I headed downstairs to switch the laundry over. Joe had arrived at my parents' house but I hadn't heard him follow me down. I bent and hauled a long string of wet clothes out of the washer, bent again to put them in the dryer. Then I felt someone lift and turn me. Joe was sliding me on top of the dryer. I sat facing him and we looked at each other. He touched my face but didn't say anything. Then

I put my mouth to his and he was exactly how I had imagined him: confident, precise, and hungry, as if for once we could stop competing. Here was a win we could share.

6

PEOPLE OF THE LAND

EVERY JEWISH CONVERT has a sponsoring rabbi. Mine was Illana Schwartz of Temple Emanu-El in West Lafayette, Indiana, a slender, freckled-faced woman with unusually large feet, who in nearly every sense proved to be the opposite of Reverend Ron Findley.

Wherever the rabbi went a noiselessness seemed to envelop her. Whisking through the temple halls on Shabbat eve in her white robes, or during the week when I often found her in her office reading, she had about her a solemn quiet that came across as unwelcoming but authentic, not directed at anyone but a natural way of existing in the world.

Rabbi Schwartz rarely smiled. The single exception to this was when her husband and children filed in a few moments before Friday evening services began. Week in and week out, her face lit up at the sight of them, but otherwise she was so serious that I often wondered if this characteristic was learned or innate. As a member of one of the only branches of Judaism that ordained women, she had good reason not to smile much at work. Rabbi Schwartz was relatively young, a woman in her early forties, and smiling could be perceived as a negation of expertise, a nullification of the few gray strands flecking her short black hair.

On the only other occasion that Rabbi Schwartz did smile—oddly, in a picture snapped right after my conversion—she looked girlish. Perhaps, then, not smiling was Rabbi Schwartz's studied way of appearing, at all times, as old and wise as the best of them.

And she was.

After graduating from the University of Houston, I completed the bulk of my conversion work at Purdue. Shortly after my interview with the bet din and my immersion in the mikveh, Rabbi Schwartz and I met in her office. It was April and I was graduating in May with my master's degree. I felt light on my feet, having completed my conversion and finished my master's. The rabbi asked me about my plans after graduation.

"I don't know. I may go back to Michigan."

"Detroit?" Rabbi Schwartz stood to open the blinds.

"No, Ludington."

"Ludington? I've never heard of it."

"There's some openings at a small college there, part-time. For me and my boyfriend."

"Joe?" She sat back down. "Is there a local temple?"

"No."

Rabbi Schwartz shifted her gaze from mine. She put her hands together, lifted them, looked back out the window, and scooted her chair closer to her desk. Inwardly I winced, imagining what she was thinking. What person, in their right mind, would work for years to become Jewish and then just go off with some schmuck who wasn't?

"The closest temple is an hour south of Ludington," I offered.

"That's a long drive."

"I know. Rabbi, it's not like we're going to stay there."

"Hmm. And do you plan on staying with Joe?"

I thought about the question. A month earlier Joe had cut his hair. After thirteen years in the making, his dreadlocks were gone, buzzed off. Why? Because we were going to visit my Southern Baptist grandparents after graduation.

"Yes," I said.

The rabbi and I were silent for a long moment. Then the conversation stumbled on, to the upcoming observance of Passover and the various spring activities of the temple's Sisterhood group. Later, when I got up to leave, Rabbi Schwartz walked me out.

"This is our final meeting," she told me at the door. "Since your conversion is complete, there's no need for ongoing sponsorship. In Judaism, after one's conversion is complete, it's disrespectful to classify them as convert." She turned to look squarely at me. "You are now, simply, always, a Jew. Remember that."

I was caught off guard, not having realized this would be our final meeting.

"Oh." I fought the urge to embrace her. "Thank you for everything, Rabbi."

I opened the temple door and walked out.

"One last thing," Rabbi Schwartz called, "to remember."

"Yes?"

"Even secular Jews, those who don't practice, know the benefits of being among those who do. They know it's good to have a community, a local temple." The rabbi paused. "Think of how the *Sh'ma* begins, Ruth."

The Sh'ma, the universal Jewish prayer recited by many upon waking and before sleeping, over children at bedtime, on Shabbat and High Holy Days, was one I knew by heart.

"Sh'ma Yisrael."

Rabbi Schwartz took a few steps out of the temple toward me. "Precisely. It doesn't begin with a call to God. It starts *Hear, O Israel.* Hear, my people. Our fundamental prayer begins as a summons to other Jews. For your own sake, I'd make every effort to find them."

☾

AT THE BEGINNING of July, one month after moving into Replica Dodge, I agreed to care for a friend's property. She and her husband were going on vacation with their boys, Jen called to say, and she trusted me with the house, land, and animals.

"Think of it as your formal introduction to the country," she said.

After weeks of being wound tight, trying to adjust to the slowness of daily life on a dirt road, the idea of a "formal introduction" held instant appeal. I immediately agreed. If anything could convince me of the possibility of ever feeling at home in Mason County, I'd find it on Jen and Paul's picturesque ten-acre plot.

Jen and Paul owned an immaculate Amish-built three-story, two rescue dogs, seven cats, and sixteen chickens, and their property embodied everything favorable people imagine about living in the country before actually moving there, before understanding what keeping up a property like that entails. In the previous months, as Joe and I house-hunted, dinners at Jen and Paul's had encouraged us to keep driving away from the lake, further east from Ludington, until we hit on Replica Dodge.

There was the distinct sense, during every visit, that our friends had mastered the art of rural life. They grew strawberries, raised animals, took in strays, and kept their south field mowed. Their kitchen window overlooked a pasture path. Their porch swing swayed in a strong breeze. Even the position of their house was picturesque: cresting a small hill, it stood sublimely on its modest green peak.

As a professor of communications, Jen caught signals in conversation other people missed. This was something I noticed from the start. Cuing into the verbal and nonverbal was part of her expertise, but it was more than a career field for Jen—it was genetic. Thirteen years older, she was thirty-nine when we first met. Her straight dark hair, bordering on black, hung in stark contrast to her blue eyes. A Mason County native, she had grown up on her family's dairy farm, which had resulted in a hardness in Jen that was common in Michigan farm kids. She'd done her share of midnight milkings, but there was also a worldliness about her: she had studied in Detroit, had spent a summer at Oxford, and had lived in Minneapolis, Milwaukee, and Boca Raton, Florida. She'd gone out and come back.

Our friendship began soon after Joe and I moved to Mason County, when Jen offered me rides home from the college on Wednesday afternoons to the cottage Joe and I were renting. The following summer, as Joe and I began to search for our own property, Jen and I had started running together on the hills surrounding her homestead.

That's when I first came to delight in watching her chickens waddle about and scratch the earth. Jen and Paul kept heritage hens.

Golden-laced wyandotte, buff Brahma, black Australorp, Araucana, and bantams, breeds with poetry-in-motion names and flamboyant feathers. Except for the five bantams, who stayed pint-sized throughout their lives, all of them were fat, having had the luxury to heft up as sources of eggs rather than meat.

On that first evening after Jen's family left on vacation, I pulled into the gravel drive with Joe. The chickens, pinheads down and wings tight around their rumps, raced to greet us.

"They know a dinner bell," Joe mumbled.

I climbed out and the chickens formed a loose huddle around me, trailing me into the barn. We came out again as a group, and as I sprinkled the feed over the grass as Jen had shown me, they darted about, squabbling. I waited for the larger ones to begin eating before feeding the smaller ones.

In the coop, drawing the eggs up from the straw, I was surprised by how warm they were, like stones left in high sun. I took them into the house and gently washed them, placing them one by one in a bowl full of water to determine their freshness, as Jen had taught me. Each one sank to the bottom, an indication that they were as fresh as they would get. A feeling of satisfaction and relief rushed over me.

☾

EACH MORNING JOE and I returned to the peace of Jen and Paul's, feeding and watering the chickens who danced at the sight of us, walking the dogs, visiting the cats. In this way the tension finally broke between us. We even began talking of owning our own brood of chickens at Replica Dodge.

"Bill's church would be perfect for them," Joe said.

"Yeah. I can see those hens full to the brim. Filing out from under the wooden cross like churchgoers after a Sunday potluck."

Every evening, like clockwork, the chickens headed home to their coop, waddling up the ramp and squeezing through the small door on the side.

One morning, gathering eggs, I thought again about the strange notion that had occurred to me only a few weeks before, this idea of modern American Jews living in the country. Country Jews still seemed like a non sequitur—there was something impossible about those two words stuffed together in a single phrase, something vaguely pathetic, untenable, and funny all at once, like a joke. Like that old TV show *The Beverly Hillbillies*, only in reverse: *The Lone Jew of Mason County*.

Maybe my life had become that joke. But when would I start laughing?

One would have to go a long way back in Jewish history to find my people working the land, collecting eggs like this. That much I knew. But at some point Jews had been country people. I thought of Ruth, my namesake, affectionately referred to as the first convert. Ruth, author of those famous lines: "Do not ask me to leave you, to return from following you, for wherever you go, I will go, and wherever you lodge, I will lodge; your people shall be my people and your God my God."

If only becoming Jewish were so simple today.

I collected another egg and finished the other chores. Heading home to Replica Dodge, I was still thinking about Jews living in the country. I parked and went into the farmhouse, and for the first time since unpacking, I picked up my Torah from our living room hutch. I had intentionally placed it there, on display with my other Jewish items, my prayer book, my *menorah*, a *mezuzah*, and my set of *kiddush* cups, all serving as signposts to anyone who walked through our door that this was a Jewish home. My Torah was a thick, beautiful book, with Hebrew gold lettering over a blue cloth cover. It had been a gift from Rabbi Schwartz upon my conversion. I sat down and turned to the book of Ruth.

There it was: the tale of Ruth just as I had recalled it. Ruth gleaning the fields at the barley harvest, Ruth gathering wheat behind the reapers, Ruth going to the threshing floor. This was a Jewish tale of famine, death, conversion, journeying, and—of all things—farming.

Here, I told myself, was a simple but profound fact. The Jews of the Torah farmed the land. The Torah is replete with agrarian anecdotes, advice, warnings, and analogies. In that famous exodus, Moses does not promise to bring the Jewish slaves of Egypt to a great city full of job opportunities, but to "a land flowing with milk and honey." The word *field* even appears in the Commandments (Thou shall not covet thy neighbor's wife—or field).

I closed the book, running my fingers over the Hebrew lettering. I kissed the spine, a gesture I had learned in services years ago, and placed it back on the hutch. Why were there so few rural traces left? In the thousands of years since the Torah was written, how had the Jews become associated almost exclusively with urban life? What had happened to Jewish farming? Why was I the Lone Jew of Mason County?

☾

ON THE SIXTH night of caring for Jen and Paul's property, I arrived later than usual to shut the chickens in. There was a dark cloudless sky above me. The moon was waxing. I was thankful that night, looking up at it, because it was the first time I was alone in the rural dark and not frightened. I peeked inside the coop and saw it full, the hens nestled up against one another, cooing at my presence. I scanned Jen's yard for any remaining chickens, closed the side door to the coop, and drove back to Replica Dodge.

The next morning Joe was inside their house leashing the dogs when I saw it. I stopped and stared. The color raged against the light concrete near the feed bag. There was a thin wash of blood at my feet. I peered at it. Had it always been there? Hadn't I seen it before? I stepped further into the barn.

There the blood was pooled. Broad flanks of skin, feathers still attached, curled up on the floor, pale as onion peels. I crouched down, taking in the scene, unbelievable even as it spread before me, then something went wrong in my legs. I couldn't stand again. Pink entrails stretched across Jen and Paul's wood pile, untangled into wet ropes of gut. Feathers coated the barn's corners, the bucket of rakes, and even the feed bag itself, where the grain had spilled out onto the floor.

I had forgotten to close the barn door.

I had closed the coop but not the barn.

Oh, God, I thought, frantic. Some of the chickens must have nestled down for the night there. This was completely my fault. They had been dragged off. Long streaks of blood extended into the furthest recesses of the barn. I forced myself up and forward, then turned and stumbled back. Again I tried to force forward, to see what was left, but true to my city roots, I took off running in the opposite direction, back toward the house. I screamed for Joe, who burst out of the front door and came racing to me. All I could do was point.

At the back of the barn were four hens, heads ripped clean off.

☾

"Raccoons," Jen said when I called her.

She was visiting Frank Lloyd Wright's Falling Waters, which somehow made me feel even worse. Here I was bringing news of a chicken massacre as she stood in the masterpiece of an architect who believed man's best friend was the tree.

Shit, I thought. Shit.

I told her the facts. "Four are dead, one is missing. All bantams. I'm so sorry, Jen."

The image of her youngest son, Thomas, pained me. Not two weeks earlier, after raising the new flock, he had released the bantams to join the larger heritage breeds. Not a month before that, he had selected from among the bevy of chicks screeching under the heat lamp the tiniest chick I had ever seen, gently picking it up from the sawdust-layered washtub set up in their basement. Thomas had placed the chick in my hand, showing me how to hold the creature, how to support its claws and body. How to make it feel warm and secure.

Jen's lack of shock astonished me. She was not happy, but she was not shocked. "It's the country," she said. "These things happen."

From the kitchen window overlooking the pasture path, I watched Joe carry the carcasses into the tall grass beyond the compost pile. A neck hung over the side of his shovel.

"I'm so sorry, Jen. I'm so sorry."

Joe dumped the carcasses onto the grass and jumped on the shovel, sinking the blade in far in the first dig.

"Stop apologizing. Death is a shadow in the country, you need to know that. Living in it means accepting fatalities."

☾

WE ROUNDED OUT the week at Jen and Paul's but the welcome to the country I had needed, the hope I had been waiting for, seemed snatched back from my grasp. A bright sadness tumbled toward me in the coming days. Jen forgave my neglect. Our friendship was easily salvaged, but the bantam massacre had sealed something for me. These hills could never be home. Something about me was at odds with the Michigan countryside, something fundamental.

Maybe, I kept thinking, Jews had good reasons for leaving this life behind.

Rabbi Schwartz was right. It was far simpler to engage in a tradition when immersed, when being with other Jews was an environmental constant rather than an uncommon treat. I hated to admit I was starting to forget the structure of even a basic Sabbath service, the songs, the prayers in Hebrew. For my own sake, I should have made every effort to find a community. I should have listened to her. I should never have come to Mason County.

With my optimism dissolving into sadness and my sadness swelling into anger, I spent the next few days deep in research at the college's library. Now more than ever I needed the answer to the question I had been asking all week. With such a rich agricultural history, why had the Jews stopped farming?

Was it because of what I had once heard, that at certain points throughout history, Jews had been prohibited from owning property? Or was it tied to something else I'd picked up—that at some point, Jews were restricted to positions of money lending and so, by occupational segregation, were constrained to European cities? What could this history tell me about my own failure, so far, to adjust to life in Mason County?

Eventually I came across an article by Maristella Botticini and Zvi Eckstein in the *Journal of the European Economic Association.* I was surprised by what I learned. According to Botticini and Eckstein's research, none of my original speculations were remotely accurate. None could account for why Jews had abandoned agrarian life. This involved a history reaching further back than the European Middle Ages, and it had little to do with occupational segregation or land-owning restrictions. It had everything to do with life in ancient Jerusalem.

☾

THE SECOND DESTRUCTION of the Temple in Jerusalem instigated a sea change in Judaism, causing a certain subsection of Jewish leaders (known as the Pharisees) to understand something beyond a shadow of a doubt. For Judaism to survive, it could no longer rely on a single venue to serve as the centerpiece of religious life. By 70 CE the great Temple had been destroyed not once, but twice, and the Pharisees knew the Jews needed something else to anchor them as a people. This is when the Torah, full of history and commandments, love songs and family lineages, emerged as a natural surrogate.

But there was a catch. If the Torah was going to become central to Jewish life, the Pharisees reasoned, its followers needed to know how to read it. This was a radical idea. As Botticini and Eckstein point out, the Christian Bible was not translated into the vernacular for another thousand years. Common literacy was unheard of, and yet in the decades after 70 CE, the Pharisees began a campaign for every Jewish man to learn to read. The sea change was under way.

Common literacy was an extraordinarily tall order for the existing Jewish population, most of whom were subsistence farmers, but the Pharisees charged ahead, championing scholars and teachers and encouraging the erection of synagogues, those houses of study and worship, in lieu of the original Temple in Jerusalem. For the Pharisees, the survival of Judaism depended on people's ability to read and discuss its holy text. No Torah, no Jews.

Yet for scores of illiterate Jewish farmers, education remained prohibitively expensive. Many found themselves lost in that sea change's simple economics, unable to pay for a son's education, let alone their own. Nor could they afford to migrate to areas where growing Jewish populations—cities in the making—meant that synagogues were being built, and that the cost of literacy was lower.

To these Jewish farmers, education was a far-flung possibility. After all, one did not need to know how to read to work the land. Botticini and Eckstein describe how the Hebrew term *ammei ha-aretz* also changed during these years. Originally meaning "people of the land"—a simple description of one's trade—after 70 CE, the phrase morphed. With the Pharisees' literacy campaign gaining widespread acceptance, *ammei ha-aretz* shifted from a vocation, from "I farm," to a slur of sorts. By 200 CE it was a term reserved for Jews who had failed to educate their sons in the very act designed to keep Judaism alive: learning to read.

For these subsistence farmers, unable to pay for a son's education, illiterate themselves, one appealing option was conversion. A movement within Judaism, albeit one heading toward the fringe, offered a religion of faith and prayer with no additional educational requirement. After 70 CE, as common literacy took off, conversion took hold in the rural stretches between larger Jewish settlements.

These Jews were choosing Christianity.

☾

FOUR DAYS AFTER returning from vacation, Jen called me. At the sound of the ringing phone, I had had the usual three seconds to bolt from the farmhouse and reach the part of the yard where I got service. Standing outside half dressed, I was betting on no one driving past Replica Dodge. It was a warm Wednesday morning in mid-July, and this time, it was Jen who sounded frantic.

"My cat may have rabies."

"What?"

"A bat flew into my house last night. The cat caught it. There's bat blood on the bathroom floor."

"Is the bat dead?"

"No. Injured. I've got to catch and kill it."

"What?"

"I have to catch and kill it because the health department only accepts dead animals for testing."

I pictured the small wounded animal fluttering about her house, disoriented and exhausted in the light of day. Another death on the farm. I flinched. But why had Jen called me?

"Where is it? Where are you?"

"It's crawling up the curtains in the library. It gets up a few feet and falls back down—"

"How are you going to kill it?"

"I've got a tennis racket, but if that doesn't work, with ether," she said. "Never mind the bat. The real reason I'm calling is to see if you want to go to the vet with me. Because now I have to take the cat to the vet to have him tested for rabies."

"You have to have them both tested? The cat and the bat? Which cat?"

"Tarragon."

Then Jen's voice broke. I had never heard her cry before, and this sudden plunge into softness floored me.

"Are you okay?"

There was a silence during which I knew Jen was trying to regain her composure.

"Yes. Maybe. It depends on how Tarragon's test comes back."

Another silence. Then she spoke again. "Michigan law stipulates that any animal positive for rabies must be euthanized."

☾

WE WERE SPEEDING down the interstate at seventy miles an hour when Tarragon the cat jimmied out of his backseat carrier and started freely roaming Jen's car. The tomcat had been antsy, howling, but now his freedom quieted him. It was raining hard and the July thunderstorm transformed the car windows into studies of blurred and dragging color, white-gray, blue, red in fits and starts from the lights zooming past us as Jen pulled onto the shoulder and flipped on her hazards.

Jen eased Tarragon back into his carrier as rain soaked the back of her slacks. When the cat was secured once more, I studied his face. Did Tarragon have rabies? Or was he just agitated by the confinement?

I had not asked for details about the fate of the bat. Especially after the bantam massacre, I didn't want to know. Knowing the bat was dead and dropped off for testing at Mason County Health Department was enough. Now Jen faced seven days of worry as she waited for the results of the rabies test. A positive result meant that Tarragon, if he also tested positive, would be put to sleep.

In the vet's office in New Era, I sat in the waiting room. Why, I wondered, had Jen picked me to accompany her? It hadn't been a week since I had killed her chickens. You would think I'd be the last person she'd want to see right now, that she'd still be angry with me, but she wasn't—never mind the chickens, never mind the bat—more than anything she was now scared for Tarragon, her cat.

A pair of spotted hounds came through the front door with their owner, a man decked out in camouflage hunting gear, and Jen emerged from the back of the office. Her face was full of fear. For all her years on her parents' dairy farm, for all her firm reassurances that fatalities were just a part of life in the country, now it looked like it was all she could do not to weep at the checkout.

Jen paid the bill and we exited.

"I was right," she told me as we got back in the car. "If Tarragon comes back positive for rabies, he's done. It's state law."

I didn't know what to say. In what had become a refrain that month, I apologized again.

We wound back through town toward the highway. The hard storm had wrung itself out, and in the tense quietness of the car—Tarragon at last resigned to his carrier—I thought about Jen's other dogs and cats. The ones I had taken care of while she was away. They were all named for spices: Clove, Curry, Fennel, Sage.

Maybe that was it. Maybe this was why Jen was taking this situation so hard. None of those other animals—not the bantam chickens nor the bat—had been named. Not like Tarragon, whose life was now on the line. In Houston I had grown up with pets, not livestock, not wild things. I had grown up with animals we treated like family, but now I realized that this was not Jen's experience.

Some animals on her ten-acre plot were more valuable to her than others.

Suddenly Jen veered into the parking lot of a local farm market. LEWIS FARM MARKET, exclaimed the white sign beneath the entrance. HOMEMADE FUDGE, PRODUCE, & PETTING ZOO.

"I could use something sweet," she said.

As we climbed out of the car, I caught a glint of green shining through the fog that had followed the rain. There was a peacock sitting against the building's board-and-batten siding, keeping dry under the market awning. I stared at him and he stared back. His slim neck was drawn, tilted like a question mark. "That's a peacock!" I exclaimed.

"Yeah. They've had him for a while."

"Does he have a name?"

Jen shrugged. As we shuffled past him on the porch, he remained sitting.

Inside the fruits of the farm market rivaled the bird's resplendence. Deep crimson cherries, orange-gold plums, Jersey blueberries. We were the only customers. At the fudge counter, Jen purchased a pair of thick bars for the ride home.

We didn't know then that in a week's time Jen would hear from the Mason County Health Department. The bat had tested negative for rabies. Tarragon's quarantine would be abruptly and joyfully ended, and the following Saturday night, beers in hand, Jen and I would lean on the hitching post outside her Amish three-story, thankful and relieved.

"To the bat," Jen would say, raising her glass. "And his rabies-free lifestyle."

"To the bat."

That afternoon, as we left the Lewis Farm Market, I sank my teeth into a plum. The flesh fell away from the pit in a single bite. The fruit was superb: sweet-tart, a small comfort on one otherwise rotten day. Maybe this was the real welcome to the country I needed, I thought. An education, a realistic look at life here. Maybe that's why Jen had brought me along.

As I relished the rest of the plum, I had to admit that I wanted to believe some hope remained, despite everything that had happened that July. Despite accidentally killing my best friends' chickens, despite learning that the ancient Jews had chosen city life under the guidance of the Pharisees. Despite everything that had happened since I'd accepted Joe's proposal and we'd moved to Replica Dodge, I wanted to believe there was still some promise that Mason County was a place I could learn to live with, even as a modern practicing Jew.

As we headed back to the parking lot, I kept my eye out for the peacock. He had disappeared from under the awning. I was disappointed to see no sign of him, but then—just as we merged back onto the highway—I caught one final glimpse. He had gone around the corner of the market and was pecking at the dirt, weaving in and out of a herd of fenced goats. Again he came to me as a flash of green, sudden and at home.

7

APPLES DIPPED IN HONEY

ALONG THE PORCH the hollyhocks hung low in the wet cool mornings. On the property's ancient vines concord grapes grew in bunches, ripening with the approaching harvest. Four months had passed since we had moved to Replica Dodge and summer was turning to autumn. A month earlier Joe had felled a dying spruce behind the house, and now he spent hours burning the brush down to a thick white ash that swirled out from the barrel, blanketing the fire pit beyond the saloon.

There must be exceptions, I kept thinking. Practicing Jews like me, living in the country. If, almost two thousand years ago, by embracing common literacy, the Jews had transformed themselves from farmers to city dwellers, exceptions had to exist, then and now.

My research continued into September as I went looking for narratives like my own. Jews away from Jews. Jews who practiced without a community. Jews confronted with the choice of belonging to a congregation a good distance away or none at all. I read about the short-lived renaissance of Jewish farming in America during the early 1900s, and I found out about Max Yasgur, who in 1969 hosted Woodstock on his dairy farm in Bethel, New York. I read about another New York State native, Rabbi Rafoel Franklin, who had given up urban life to farm in the Catskills. "I never expected I would farm full-time," Franklin told a reporter from *Tablet Magazine* in 2011. "But *baruch Hashem*, if you do it properly, farming is the most fulfilling life I could imagine."

But none of these narratives captured my attention quite like the tales about a more unnerving subject, one Josephine Sarah Marcus Earp. Out in Replica Dodge, a small sign in the shape of an arrow stood away from the buildings. On it, in western-styled scrawl, Bill Broadwell had painted a single name: Wyatt Earp.

Wyatt Earp had been Josephine's husband. I sat on the porch holding Josephine's memoir, a book called *I Married Wyatt Earp*. A striking black-and-white photogravure graced the cover. It was Josephine as a young woman, at least according to her biographer. In that image she looks down at the lens positioned beneath her. The single item of clothing she wears is a sheer black veil, draped across her brow. The garment washes over her shoulders, full breasts, and down her body. As I had for several evenings, I studied the cover for a long time before opening the book.

Direct, vacant, unapologetic of her own nakedness, Josephine stared back at me.

☾

ACCORDING TO HARRIET Rochlin, author of *Pioneer Jews*, Josephine was "long on daring, short on propriety, and, of all things,

Jewish." She was born in 1861 to Prussian immigrants, who relocated from Brooklyn to San Francisco, where she lived until she was seventeen. Hungry for adventure, Josephine ran away to join the Pauline Markham Theater Company as a dancer. When the traveling troupe headed east into the territory of Arizona, Josephine "fell in" with Johnny Behan, a bankrupt politico, but not long afterward she caught the eye of Wyatt Earp in Tombstone.

Rochlin describes Wyatt Earp as "thirtyish, tall, handsome, and laconic." Like Josephine, the famed marshal of the true Dodge City led a life engulfed in myth. Beyond his policing duties at Dodge City, Wyatt was also purportedly a horse thief, a brothel strongman, and a notorious gambler, and as far as I could tell, the basic facts of both lives remained sketchy. But two things were certain. First, Wyatt Earp married a Jewish woman. Second, despite never converting to Judaism himself, after crisscrossing the American West with Josephine (or Sadie, as he called her) for over fifty years, Wyatt Earp died and was buried in a Jewish cemetery.

Self-reliant, full of wanderlust, equipped with a fluid set of principles that were adaptable to present circumstances, Wyatt Earp seemed to embody everything about the West people like Bill nostalgically envisioned, regardless if it was actually accurate. I looked out at the little sign with Wyatt's name scrawled on it and wondered if Bill's knowledge extended to the quieter facts of his icon's life. Did Bill know about Josephine, her Jewishness?

Summer ending meant Rosh Hashanah was coming. In mid-September Jews the world over would mark a new year. They would gather in synagogues, light candles, recite kiddush over braided *challah* loaves and kosher wine. Later some would find the shore of a sea, a river, or a lake to perform *tashlik,* a prayer of humility that ends with the symbolic gesture of emptying one's pockets into the water. *Lshanah Tovah*, they'd say, embracing: *For a good year.* Symbolic foods would be featured at the festival meal, among them apples dipped in honey. I pictured other Jews, shofars ringing out in the large congregations of Boston, New York, Chicago, the call of the ram's horn cutting through the brisk city air.

In the Jewish calendar, Rosh Hashanah not only commemorates a new year, it begins a ten-day period of self-reflection called the Days of Awe. After experiencing the warmth and joy of Rosh Hashanah celebrations, those practicing move on to the serious work of taking stock of one's life over the previous twelve months. What grudges are being clung to? Who deserves a sincere apology? What are the ways that we have "missed the mark" with ourselves, with others, with God? For the nine days that follow Rosh Hashanah, Jews are encouraged to focus on prayer, repentance, good deeds, and making amends.

The final Day of Awe is Yom Kippur, the Day of Atonement. Excluding the Sabbath, which happens weekly, this is the holiest day in the Jewish calendar, and a holiday when many Jews—even those who do not practice—turn up at the synagogue. Perhaps this is due to a comically harsh folktale relating that during the Days of Awe, God is busy inscribing people's names into the Book of Life or the Book of Death. Who lives and who dies in the coming year is decided by God during this period. Naturally it seems like a good time to show up at services.

That September, as the Days of Awe drew near, I found myself mentally circling Josephine, her story, that brazen cover image. There was something about her that stayed with me, or at least, with Replica Dodge facing my front door, it was hard not to be reminded of her.

In the years she spent far from her parents and siblings, to what extent had she felt Jewish? Had she tried to sustain a kosher diet as a traveling dancer in Markham's troupe? The thought was like a punch line. Had she said prayers, in private, each Sabbath? Maybe not. Maybe when she ran away from San Francisco, Josephine had also tried to abandon her Jewish identity.

After a long life stitched together by myth and fact, in 1944 Josephine Sarah Marcus Earp died. She was buried with her husband in the Hills of Eternity Cemetery in Colma, California, in the Marcus family plot, where her parents and siblings surround her and Wyatt to this day. Colma is twelve miles south of San Francisco, the city Sadie had fled at seventeen, and this was something else that stayed with me. In her last years, Sadie had gone home. She had crisscrossed the American West only to return to California. Which means that at some point, arguably, between boomtowns and gunfights, Josephine had grown weary and homesick. She had started longing for the community—the Jews—she once knew.

☾

CONSTRUCTED IN 1886, ten years before the farmhouse, the barn at Replica Dodge features hand-hewn crossbeams. In the century-plus since its construction, its siding boards have inched further and further apart. At dusk the sun pours through those gaps in broad ribbons of light, and on any clear evening, I learned that September, if I stayed in the barn long enough, I could watch that light arcing across the floor with the setting of the sun.

But the evening before Rosh Hashanah wasn't clear. It was storming. I stood in our barn listening for leaks. Jen had told me that most barns are made or broken by the quality of the roof, by how much water it does or does not let in. Remnants of a few hay bales spilled over a high loft. The rain pounded against the galvanized steel above me and made it sound as if I were standing inside a great drum. While the barn wasn't warm, it was dry.

It was also a holy mess. Every trinket, knickknack, tool, or antique Bill had bought but hadn't used in Replica Dodge, he had heaped into grand piles in the barn. When we bought the property, we assumed these masses would disappear by the time we moved in. Not so. It wasn't entirely uncommon, we learned later, for people to leave whatever was in the barn as both gift and burden to the newcomers.

In our case that meant moth-eaten bags of *TV Guides*, fake Christmas trees, stacks of small clay pots, boxes of Miracle-Gro, dollar-store lawn ornaments, busted boat motors, bent fishing poles, TV antennas, mason jars, antique wagon wheels, wire animal traps, metal gas cans, plastic bread bins, coils of defunct hose, red bricks, rusted-out shovels and broken rakes, and every variety of pulverized lawn chair imaginable.

On Rosh Hashanah I had planned to go into Ludington to book the Stearns Motor Inn, a historical hotel, for our wedding reception. Joe and I had set a date for the next June and Stearns was as close to perfect as we could afford for our medium-sized party. The hotel ballroom offered air-conditioning, hardwood floors, ample dancing space, and an open bar at an approachable price. Already we had decided to have our ceremony at home—not in Replica Dodge or the farmhouse, but in a nearby meadow owned by the Skiptons—but if it rained, Stearns would allow us to host the ceremony there.

I attach some degree of luck to wedding ceremonies held at personal residences because my parents had married at their house in

Houston. My mother liked to brag that they had spent less than two hundred dollars on the whole affair, a second marriage for them both. My mother in a dress from Foley's, my father fully bearded, they got married in front of the fireplace. As a girl I'd seen pictures of them rushing out of our house to "who knows where," as my mother liked to tell it, her southern accent at full tilt. "We hadn't planned a honeymoon. We just realized people expected us to leave at some point, so we did. We drove around and around, not sure where to end up, until we found this place called the Pecker Motel." Then she'd laugh and slap the countertop.

I smiled anytime I thought of that story, but there was another, more practical reason to host our ceremony near Replica Dodge: the closest synagogue was over an hour's drive south. It seemed unreasonable to ask guests who were traveling from Texas, Washington, New York, or New Mexico to spend yet another hour on the road.

That was the plan, but then Joe had said something, and this was why I was standing in our barn during a storm the night before Rosh Hashanah, listening and looking for leaks. He had suggested holding the reception inside the barn.

"We'll rip out the cabinets, tear down the workshop, clean it all up. We can lap over the floorboards," he said. "We could do it before June. Get the barn back to its good bones."

I frowned. "I thought we'd agreed on Stearns."

"Yeah." Joe cleared a path through the piles. "Just think about it."

I tried to imagine it then, the barn without its junk. Despite its heaps, I had to admit it had a certain charm. It had kept its good shape and scent, was sturdy and smelled inviting, like walnuts toasting in a warm oven. In an odd way, there was something vaguely fetching about the idea.

It had become fashionable for urbanites to host wedding receptions in renovated barns, something that people from Mason County had been doing for centuries. The major difference, of course, was that these city couples rented their barn space. They rented the rural experience. This was our barn. Scanning the piles again, I knew that preparing for such a crowd would be a massive undertaking. Was there time? Was there enough money?

One way or another, we would eventually have to deal with the piles.

"Okay," I told Joe later that evening. "Let's renovate it."

Even as the barn stood submerged in dollar-store trinkets, the space was not so unlike a sanctuary. High ceilings, bare beams. I kept going back to the way that sunlight moved through it on clear evenings. It reminded me of my favorite place in the world: Houston's Rothko Chapel.

☾

AFTER MY FAMILY relocated to Alpena during my freshman year of college, I started spending Sunday afternoons in the Rothko. For a long stretch before that I had not attended church, and I had not missed much about it either, because it was difficult to miss what one couldn't relate to, and after exposing my doubts to Reverend Findley, after not being confirmed, after sitting in the front row with the entire congregation at my back, I wanted nothing to do with church.

But when my parents left for Michigan, suddenly I couldn't go home. Not on weekends, not ever. Even though it was only a few minutes' drive north of the city, I couldn't go back to that house where my parents had married in front of the fireplace. They weren't there, which was as strange as it was sad, so on weekends I found myself rambling around Houston, exploring the city, trying to fill the time before classes resumed on Monday.

It was around then that I started regularly dropping in on Houston's art district, the Menil Collection and the Cy Twombly Gallery, and this is how I first stumbled into the Rothko Chapel, a humble and low building made out of tan brick. I remember that on my initial visit a woman stationed in the foyer offered me a pamphlet but said nothing. She pointed to a sign near the door of the sanctuary that encouraged silence. Not quietness, I read, but silence. I opened the door and went inside.

There, hanging like sleeping giants in the hexagonal sanctuary, were Mark Rothko's seven gigantic paintings. I knew of Rothko's work—my parents had framed a silk print of his and hung it in our kitchen. I knew that Rothko was a minimalist interested in color contrast, but I had never seen anything like this. At first sight the vast pieces appeared uniformly black. As in the barn, the only light in the chapel was natural and came from above, where a skylight allowed the sun through at sharp angles.

The place was austere and beautiful but its true splendor became visible only after my eye had time to adjust. As anyone who has spent more than ten minutes in the Rothko knows, given enough time, other shades emerge from beneath the black. Sit long enough on the plain benches staring into those paintings and all at once, Rothko's purples and reds appear. Vacillating, vanishing with the changing light.

Every Sunday I returned it was a different place. If the sky was stormy the undulations in Rothko's paintings were almost imperceptible. I would have to look for a long time to see anything but darkness. But on clearer days, when clouds moved across the sun, the scene became far more dramatic: the sanctuary dimming, the paintings pulling back into themselves, only to be lit up again, moments later, with sunlight. Then the witnessing started over. The waiting and watching, the search for Rothko's reds and purples.

In these moments it was as if I was in conversation with something or someone. The both of us present, wordless, and speaking. It was the same feeling I'd had years before, sitting in that confirmation classroom at Wildwood Methodist. At the Rothko, whatever had held me back from Christianity revealed itself again and again, upon every return. Over and over, in the plain gray room with its enormous black paintings, the old friend spoke.

It made sense that there was work involved in invoking this feeling. That one had to sit a long time, looking and listening. It was why, even after leaving church, I'd never been able to discard religion entirely. There was this nagging notion of mine that there was something holding the universe together. Not tightly, but just so. Not heaven or hell. Not the pearly gates version, just God: some loose stitch working in leaps and bounds. God who jumped away, impossible to access, who touched back down to run right through me. God like Rothko's reds and purples. God, who was there and gone and there again.

The Rothko Chapel was created as a spiritual landmark for people of all faiths, and available books included the Quran, the Bible, and the Torah as well as some Buddhist texts. After several Sunday afternoons at the Rothko, I signed up for a world religions course at the University of Houston, and the semester after that I enrolled in a course on Judaism.

The course on Judaism was taught by Rabbi Jeff Kleinman, a tall, warm-hearted man who required all his students to visit a local synagogue once during the semester and write about their experience. The day after I turned in my written response, Rabbi Kleinman and I happened to reach the classroom at the same time. It was well before the others arrived and he stopped me at the door. "Ruth, your response was excellent," he said. "I mean really. It blew me away."

"Thank you." I was glad to find him alone. Rabbi Kleinman held the door for us and we walked into the large empty classroom.

"I want to learn more about Judaism," I announced. I blurted this to his back. Rabbi Kleinman turned to face me, a cheerful bemusement sweeping over his face. "I mean, for myself," I continued, "not just for the class."

Rabbi Kleinman studied me for a moment. "Come to Hillel."

Hillel was the Jewish student organization on campus, part sanctuary, part student hangout. Kleinman oversaw it. I began attending Friday night services there and that year, my circle of friends became increasingly Jewish. On Rosh Hashanah, a fellow student invited me to her family's synagogue for the celebratory Shabbat Seder. She told me about the apples dipped in honey, poked fun at the Book of Life and Death, and explained how the ram's horn was blown, like a trumpet at the end of the service, blown for as long as the person had breath to sustain the ancient instrument.

As foreign as it all was, with so much of the service in Hebrew, something in me relaxed. In the coming months, the further into Judaism I traveled, the more it struck me how comfortable I was with my Jewish friends, Rabbi Kleinman, the Friday evening services, the content of the class. I began to consider that there had been a reason I refused confirmation at Wildwood Methodist. My sense of God—much of which I had felt all my life but had rediscovered at the Rothko the year before—was Jewish.

Had I always been this way? Had I been born, as the young man standing outside Hillel said, a Jewish soul to a Christian family? What was that word again? How I wished I could remember it! Or was this whole situation unspeakably inappropriate? How could I claim a culture of which I knew almost nothing, a culture to which I had zero ancestral right? It left me feeling squeamish, but here was my undeniable reality. Among Jews, I was home.

I had to talk to Rabbi Kleinman. I found him in his office.

"What brings you here, Ruth?" He was cheerful, as usual, but that day I did not return his smile.

I tried to think, very carefully, about the words I wanted to say. When spoken, finally, would they sail out of my mouth like a boat? Would they ferry me away from Christianity for good? Not being confirmed was one thing, but this was different. What about my own heritage, what about the people I loved? My family? My parents? My grandmother—my namesake?

"I want to become Jewish."

The rabbi's smile faltered. "Ah. I was wondering if you'd come to me about that."

"I think I already am Jewish. I'm sorry. I know how that sounds."

"How much time do you have before graduation?"

"What does time have to do with it? One more semester."

"It's not enough, Ruth."

"Not enough?"

"Conversion takes at least a year."

I was speechless. I kept thinking of all the people I'd seen "saved" at church in less than a minute.

Rabbi Kleinman continued. "Most sponsoring rabbis believe converts should not only regularly attend synagogue but should know Jewish history and culture as well, and at least enough Hebrew to get through services. And those are the liberal ones, Ruth. The Reform rabbis, like me. All this takes a great deal of time, more than you'd think." He paused, gesturing to the books lying open on his desk. "Look, I'm ordained and I'm still learning. The learning never stops."

By this point the bewilderment on my face must have been so clear and shining that Rabbi Kleinman had no choice but to power through the rest of his thoughts. "Above all, Ruth, conversions only take place when you both   you and your sponsoring rabbi—agree that you are ready to enter the covenant. The process takes tremendous commitment."

Stunned that conversion could possibly take years, I meandered in and out of the rest of the conversation as best I could.

Eventually Kleinman asked about my plans for graduate school. "As soon as you settle into Purdue, find a rabbi," he advised. "If you were here longer, I would be happy to sponsor you. But four months?" He shook his head.

"That's okay," I said, suddenly keen to exit. "Thank you for your time."

As I gathered my things to leave I could feel the rabbi's eyes on me. "You are a bit different," he said. I looked back at him. "We don't get many people like you. Most people convert because they're marrying a Jew."

"Really? How does that fit into what you said about being ready? About this covenant business?"

"It's a tricky issue," Kleinman acknowledged. "Increasingly congregations are accepting interfaith families, but officiating a wedding between a Jew and a non-Jew? That's tough. Intermarriage remains a contested issue among the rabbinate. Some view it as a dire threat, others as an unfortunate watering down of one's faith and culture. Others even see it as an outright betrayal. According to the most extreme version, interfaith marriage is accomplishing what Hitler could not."

For a second he was lost in thought. "Anyways, something to consider as you go forward."

Joe's face surged to the front of my mind. Recently he had emailed a picture from Michigan Tech where he was now in his senior year. "Physics Student of the Year," the subject line read. I had opened it immediately. The snapshot showed Joe and another student jointly receiving the university's award, Joe smiling, showing those crammed-together teeth, his sleeves rolled up, his skin tanned from hours outside playing soccer. A dull ache flashed through my chest. We were six months into a long-distance relationship, one we both knew was worth it.

☾

By my final years at the University of Houston I spent most of my time reading and writing for my classes. I moved into a single as soon as possible so I could study without interruption, a tiny one-room on the twenty-first floor of that high-rise dormitory overlooking southeast Houston. When I got tired of reading there, I'd go to Brasil's, a coffee shop frequented by grad students, and stay late into the night. It wasn't that I was shy or antisocial, but focused. I made the dean's list every semester, never drank, and rarely accepted invitations to parties, though at nineteen it began to dawn on me that something had changed since high school, because I was beginning to receive those invitations.

Mostly they came from classmates, although once a professor emailed to ask if I would like to come and see his "home library." When that happened, I went downtown to my salon and had my shoulder-length hair cut to within a half inch of my scalp. The male attention evaporated, which was fine with me, because by then there was only one male whose attention I craved, and he went to school half a nation away.

"I think I want to become Jewish," I said again, this time into the phone. A week after my talk with Rabbi Kleinman, I had finally summoned the courage to share my thoughts with Joe. I hated telling him this way but I had decided it couldn't wait until Christmas break. Conversations like this always seemed to highlight the thousands of miles separating us. I thought about Joe sitting in his dorm room at Michigan Tech, way up in Michigan's Upper Peninsula.

"That's weird."

"I know. It *is* weird."

I waited for him to say something else, but he didn't.

I went on. "I don't even know if they'll take me. Apparently it can take years, and it's more about a community accepting you, not the other way around."

More silence.

"Sounds like serious business," he said at last. "I guess I can't be surprised. You've been spending most of your Friday nights at services."

"There's work involved. A lot of it. According to Kleinman the process requires 'tremendous commitment.' So I need to know now if it's going to be a problem for you."

"Natalie . . ." Joe trailed off.

Oh, God, he's trying to find the right words. Congratulations, I thought to myself, you've run off the only guy you're nuts about. I bit my lip and put my forehead on the desk.

Finally Joe spoke again. "You make up your own mind. I guess I admire that about you. Even when it's not a choice I would make myself."

I hadn't realized I had been holding my breath. I exhaled. "Thanks."

"Can I ask when you're planning to tell your parents? Aren't they Southern Baptist or something?"

"Methodist, but the rest of my family is fully steeped in the Southern Baptist tradition. So I'm not going to mention it for a long time. If conversion takes years, then I'll have years to tell them."

For the first time then I considered Joe's parents. I pictured his mother, a devout Catholic who attended Mass two times a week, who had sent all her children to Catholic school, who had placed a statue of Mary, palms heavenward, in the garden at their house in Alpena.

"I really never thought about your parents," I admitted. "Do you think it will be an issue?"

"Don't count on it. Even if my parents disagreed, they would never say so. My family is not exactly known for discussing difficult topics with each other."

I persisted. "But this is something that will change me. Internally, for the most part. I'm hoping to join the most liberal branch of Judaism, so it's not as if I'll be unrecognizable. But there will be some external changes. Diet, probably. And holidays."

"Holidays stink. I mean, they're good for family and food, but they've been blown out of proportion. Seismically. Any effort that deescalates the mania surrounding your run-of-the-mill American holiday is something I can support."

I laughed. "You may find yourself celebrating new holidays."

"I'm okay with that."

I was relieved. The conversation had gone as well as I could have hoped.

"There is something you should understand."

"Oh?"

"I'm all in, Natalie. I'll support you. I'll go to services with you. I'll even celebrate holidays with you, if that's what you want. Just don't ever ask me to become Jewish."

Something in me hit a snag. Though I had never considered asking Joe to become Jewish before—for me, for us—there was something about his declaration that made me feel like I had just swallowed a rock.

For the second time since I had decided to pursue conversion a short week before, the potential pitfalls of marrying outside the faith had, circuitously, come up. Again I recalled my conversation with Kleinman: interfaith marriage as a voluntary watering down of one's faith. It did raise difficult questions. If I married Joe, would we be a Jewish family? Or a family with one Jew in it? And what if we had children? Would they be Jews?

Back up, I told myself. It's not as if he's proposed.

"Jews don't go looking for converts," I said.

"That's good. Because you know I don't believe in God. And I don't think there's anything wrong with that."

"I know." In my stomach the rock settled into place.

☾

THAT SEPTEMBER ON my runs along the country roads, I kept being reminded of Anatevka, the setting of Joseph Stein's *Fiddler on the Roof*, another narrative of Jews caught in an agrarian-based lifestyle. The Mason County fields were high with corn now, the harvest under way, and as I ran I could always count on seeing more animals than humans, herds of whitetail deer, rabbits scurrying into the brush, a flock of wild turkeys. Once, light as a ghost, I spotted a red fox fleeing into the cherry orchard.

I thought about the character of Chava, the youngest daughter of Tevye, meandering home with her milk cow on a country road like the one before me. The crunch of gravel underfoot. That sound had become intimate to me now, on these runs. In *Fiddler on the Roof* it's this scene when Chava meets Fyedka, a Russian farmer— not a Jew—the man she eventually marries. In that first encounter, Fyedka offers Chava a book. He knows she likes to read. "Let me tell you about myself," Fyedka says. "I'm a pleasant fellow. Charming, honest, ambitious, quite bright. And very modest."

In was late into the Days of Awe and though I saw Anatevka around me, I was fantasizing about a life back in Houston. Or maybe Boston, Chicago, or New York. Living in some high-rise apartment in the heart of a bustling metropolis, where each Friday night there would be the lullaby of a Shabbat service, the pure gradual darkening of a full sanctuary. A place where there would be public transportation and other neighbors who, like me, in a few short months wouldn't buy Christmas trees.

My fantasies carried on as I baked challah in the farmhouse oven and as I said the blessings alone. I lit the candles and planned a drive into Ludington, to the shore of Lake Michigan, to recite *tashlik*.

In their single, scraggly row on the extra two acres at Replica Dodge, the criterion apples had ripened from a blanched green to a blushing amber. One evening I went out and picked one, washed it under running water in the sink, cut it, and drizzled the slices with honey. I offered half to Joe. "L'shanah Tovah," I said, embracing him.

Joe was baffled. "L'shanah . . . what?"

About a month earlier we had started searching for a rabbi to officiate at our wedding. Things were off to a slow start. Rabbi Kleinman had been right. Most congregations accepted interfaith families, but officiating at a marriage between a Jew and a non-Jew remained controversial at best.

On top of this I hadn't joined a synagogue. Which one would I join, anyway, being so far away? As humiliating as it was, the month before I had started cold-calling rabbis I had never met. The outlook was bleak, but one afternoon I received a call back from Rabbi Menshov of Grand Rapids, Michigan, a midsized city two hours southeast of Replica Dodge.

We exchanged pleasantries. Then Menshov said, "I have one question for you."

"Yes?"

"Is your future husband Jewish?"

Everything in me sank. "No."

"Is he willing to convert?"

"No," I repeated. My eyes filled with tears.

"I'm sorry," Menshov said. "Then I cannot help you."

8

DEVIL'S ADVOCATE

A RAW WIND cast its net over Replica Dodge. It was October, when autumn became irrefutable, each kind of tree handling the news in its own evolved way. The cherry trees across the road were glad to oblige that wind, becoming bare seemingly a full season too soon, but the sugar maples at the entrance of our drive held their leaves, hosting grand recitals of color: coral, burnt gold, firebrick. The oaks opted for a more subtle form of acceptance, a gradual drying out and browning, as did our golden rain tree, leaves furled tight once they finally let go. The tall grasses behind the barn, once dead straight in the August heat, now huddled together like children at the bus stop trying to keep warm.

That wind found its way inside. In the early dark, our farmhouse was frigid. I found myself lingering beneath the covers with Joe. Getting out of bed stung, but getting in did too, each night the sheets just as cold as the rest of the house. We shivered and moved closer.

At the end of September we had ordered six cords of oak but didn't know if that would be enough, didn't know how quickly it would burn in the outdoor woodstove set to funnel heat into our house during the upcoming winter.

Winter. Winter. I kept rolling the word over in my mouth, as if saying it could make it more bearable or slow its advance. As if repeating meant there would be no black ice, no clouds lingering for weeks like gauze blotting out the sun. By then I had started writing something new. Not a book, not yet, but scenes engaged in the same conversation, images, utterances, cultural norms, exchanges. I was recording my first year in Mason County's countryside because I wanted to remember, I told myself, how strange it was at the start.

I knew being Jewish had something to do with the story I needed to tell.

But what was the point of writing about God in this day and age? Who would care about the inner workings of anyone's spiritual life, especially if the point wasn't to proselytize? In my mind circulated memories of the academics I had grown up among, the atheist I was about to marry. For so many of them religion had long ceased to be relevant, nothing more than a vestige of childhood from which they eagerly emerged as free-thinking, well-educated adults.

I kept writing.

☾

THAT FIRST OCTOBER in Replica Dodge, in beginning to jot down scenes and in starting to understand the story I needed to write, I knew I had to begin by reexamining my own family's history—not just my grandmother's, but also my parents' individual relationships with religion.

I needed to ask my mother about her past but I dreaded it. Not the recent past. Not even about her first marriage, decades prior, to a man named Roy, but before that. I had to ask my mother about her childhood.

I kept going back to a conversation we'd had during my teenage years, one that pointed to the extreme privilege of my own childhood in contrast to hers. My youngest years had included a father who was present, a house in the suburbs, and a smart, hardworking mother, all of which had amounted to backyard playhouses, flute lessons, piano recitals, symphonies, and art exhibits.

I prepared myself to bring up the delicate subject and waited until we were in the same room again, until my mother visited the farmhouse for the first time. One morning after Joe left for work, we found ourselves in the living room.

"It's cold in here," she said.

I retrieved a quilt from the back of a chair. "The wood is supposed to arrive any day now." Crawling under its heavy warmth, we nestled next to each other on the couch.

The time was right. In the ensuing conversation I learned that there hadn't been much in my mother's life, in terms of faith, before my sister and I were born. "Besides the gospels," my mother told me. "Those we had plenty of. My mother, your grandmother Joyce, loved Johnny Cash's take on the gospels." She paused. "Actually, after we moved into our apartment at the San Felipe Courts, we did make sure to 'affiliate' with a church. Churches gave us clothes and food. And sometimes rides." She paused, longer now. "I think I was even baptized."

"So you believed?"

"Well, I wouldn't go that far. When you grow up in the Courts and someone takes you to church for the first time . . ." She looked out the window at Replica Dodge. "They used to bus us over. Some fancy church on the north side. Everyone there was so clean and well dressed." She rolled her eyes. "They're better than you. You know it, they know it. But then they start talking . . ." She trailed off again, looking back out the window to Replica Dodge, where we had recently boarded up the saloon to keep its batwing doors from rattling back and forth in the wind.

"And you start to listen. These stories from the Bible. I mean, leprosy healed with a touch? A man walking on waves?" She shrugged. "Food for thousands, out of nothing? Come on, I couldn't believe, at least not then."

Then my mother looked at me in a way that made me want to look away. "Please," she said. "There were no miracles where I came from."

☾

THE SAN FELIPE Courts, where my mother spent her childhood, was a long series of low-income housing units located in Houston's Fourth Ward. Originally dubbed Freedmen's Town by the former slaves who had flooded the area after the Civil War, by the 1940s, right before the erection of the San Felipe Courts, the area was home to some of Houston's most prominent black neighborhoods.

According to historian Cary D. Wintz, during the early 1940s, as acres began to be cleared for the future housing project, local residents were displaced. To make matters worse, when the San Felipe Courts finally opened in 1944—first for defense workers, then for single mothers on welfare like my grandmother Joyce—

it remained segregated. The Courts admitted no members of the surrounding black community.

Once the valedictorian of her high school class, my grandmother Joyce struggled with major depression in adulthood. In 1958, when my mother was ten years old, her father abandoned the family for good, and with him went the middle-class income he earned as an exterminator. *Wine, women, and song,* my mother liked to say about her own father. I never met my grandfather, and though my mother didn't like to talk about her past, the story of his desertion was one I knew. This was how she came to spend the rest of her childhood in Houston's largest housing project.

My mother remembers rumors about the Courts having been built over a cemetery. "They just stacked us," she once told me. "Dead and alive, poor on top of poor."

When I was eleven years old, my mother took me with her downtown for "Take Your Daughter to Work Day." I was hungry for her company during those years; between her full-time job at the medical center and earning her degree at night, my mother was a busy woman. Most mornings I would wake with red lipstick on the back of my hand, where my mother had kissed me before leaving for work. But that day I was going with her.

We had left home fifteen minutes earlier than her usual departure time and I was sleepy, dozing in the passenger seat of the family Lincoln as my mother drove. I woke as she parked the car. Houston's skyline was just decipherable in the day's first light. I stared out the windshield at the place we had stopped, a seemingly never-ending rambling of low yellow-brick apartments, half demolished, their street-facing walls knocked out, levels exposed. The buildings ran down the street and out of sight. A bulldozer, its blade resting on the wet upturned dirt, was parked near one of the buildings, and a wire fence, ripped with holes, ran the length of the complex. I rubbed my eyes. The Courts first struck me as a type of prison.

"Where are we?" I asked. "Is this your work?"

"No. This is where I grew up."

She ran her hand through my hair, smoothing it. Light inched into the car. As usual, my mother's appearance was all business. Olive dress, gold belt and earrings, high pumps, manicured nails, dark hair curled. I studied her but couldn't read her mood. The expression in her eyes was relaxed but she was biting the inside of her cheek. As I gazed at her in the gray light, I recalled with regret all the people who had remarked on how much I looked like my dad. I had been hoping to inherit any scrap of my mother's good looks.

We sat for what seemed a long time. Then my mother turned the Lincoln's ignition over. "They're tearing it down," she said. "I just wanted you to see it before it's gone."

We pulled away and she didn't say anything more.

☾

GROWING UP, I gradually came to piece together that my mother's attendance at Wildwood Methodist was perfunctory, and that this had something to do with her childhood in the San Felipe Courts.

Each Sunday she would sit with the rest of the family in church, and at first I took this as proof that like everyone else in the pews around me, she had been "saved." Only as I got older—fifteen or sixteen—did her indifference clarify for me. Some evenings my father would bring the church newsletter in from the mailbox and read aloud from it: they were repainting the annex, they needed someone to chaperone a youth trip, they wanted family photos for the church directory . . . my mother would always decline. She never took Communion.

Because I sensed there was a connection between her childhood in the Courts and her religious reluctance, as I got older, I started asking her about that childhood. More often than not she would sidestep the question, but one time, I didn't let her off easy. I was sixteen and it was just the two of us eating downtown at Nit Noi, our favorite Thai restaurant. We were sharing an order of spring rolls and peanut sauce and I was pressing hard for information.

"Fine," she said. "You want to know what it was like?" She took a sip of water, leaving a halo of red lipstick on her straw. "In the 1960s, I was younger than you. I was twelve, and the gangs in the Courts were cut along racial lines." She wound the longest strands of her dark hair, marbled with gray, around her fingers. "The women in the Courts wore their hair like this." She lifted her own into a bun. "To hide their knives."

Letting her hair fall, she picked up a spring roll, dipped it in the peanut sauce, and took a bite. "I don't know what to tell you. Violence was the rule rather than the exception. Between the whites and Latinos—the only other people they allowed inside as residents, by listing them as 'whites'—fights broke out all the time. Except at night, when those from the surrounding black community crossed into San Felipe."

"What happened then?"

"The whites and Latinos got together to beat them senseless."

I stared at her.

She took another bite of spring roll. "Any other questions?"

"Were you in a gang?"

My mother shook her head. "No. But I learned to run fast. With three brothers, I just needed to get to my front door and I'd be safe. I'm done talking about this now."

I backed off then and for good. After that I quit asking about the Courts, but from time to time my mother would speak of them, in passing, a few facts slipping out with no further elaboration.

I heard the most about my mother's past when Kathy, her best friend who had grown up next door to her in the San Felipe Courts, visited us in Lexington Woods. Kathy could talk a blue streak, and she told stories of outsmarting social workers, stabbings, of my mother being hung out of a high window by her ankles. She told us of the time my mother, sixteen, skipping school to spend the day climbing the ladders at Houston's Public Library, was stopped by a modeling recruiter for Neiman Marcus, who gave her his card.

"Your mother," Kathy would say, "was always slender. And those green eyes, like bottomless wells. She was the most beautiful thing to come out of the Courts."

But it was a man named Roy, who came from Boston and had fought in Korea, who would change my mother's future for good. "He had it *made*," my mother would say then, musing with Kathy. This, I came to put together, meant he had a car. He dropped her off at school in the morning and picked her up in the afternoon, took her out to eat and to the movies—small indulgences, I imagined, that my mother could remember from when her father was still around. She was a teenager. Roy was almost thirty. He proposed.

"For all our fighting, he did get me out of that place," my mother would always say.

In 1981 she was still married to Roy when she walked into a classroom at North Harris Community College. Years had passed since she had left the Courts and now she lived a few minutes north of downtown. She was in her early thirties, and after spatting with Roy about getting a job—one she worked despite his threats—then more fighting about her going back to school, an idea he hated even more, she had finally enrolled herself in night classes.

This class, Intro to Philosophy, was taught by a young man also in his early thirties.

His name was Dr. Olin Joynton.

☾

THE REST OF US, my mother seemed to imply—my father, my sister, and I—had been raised in a way that afforded us the luxury of trusting others. Believing in happy accidents. Silver linings in tragic circumstances. And maybe, just maybe, God's greater plan.

My father, for his part, believed in family dinners. He believed in full place settings and long conversations, in putting your fork down between bites and in staying at the table until excused. This formality he had learned from his own mother, Mary Ruth, and though his parents' Depression-era childhoods made them insist their own kids finish every morsel on their plates, my father ended up average height at best.

Oddly enough, however, there was always something about my father that seemed tall. There was a natural ease and confidence in the way he moved about the world. Years later my grandmother sent us a photograph that offered one explanation for this discrepancy. It was a snapshot taken during his adolescence, when my grandfather was stationed overseas in Norway.

The photo is an outdoor shot of the Cub Scout pack Mary Ruth led in Norway, which included her young sons, Olin and Stan. There is snow on the ground and pines towering above, and the boys are lined up in sweaters and wool caps, some on skis, others in snowshoes, all posing for the camera, except two. One is a tall, blond-headed boy. He is no longer in line with the others. His head is turned and his mouth is blurred by its own movement, and he appears to be shouting at another boy, five or six boys over, who has also broken pose to glare back at him. The blond boy is husky, a full head above the others. This, I learned, was my father in 1960. Though in the coming years he would grow into a slim, dark-haired man of average height, he had once been tall compared to his peers. He had never forgotten it.

Also not forgotten: his instinct to break the line. Each Sunday evening over dinner, my father embarked on a mental exercise that as teenagers Lauren and I came to call, with equal parts affection and resentment, Devil's Advocate.

Despite my father being the single member of our family stipulating that we all go to church, marching around the house Sunday mornings keeping everyone on schedule—*You have five minutes, You have three minutes, This is your one-minute warning, Get in the car*—like clockwork, later on, his better character was restored. This was the one that stayed with us for the rest of the week. He was professorial, relaxed but never unkempt, preparing to teach philosophy the next day at the college.

"So Findley's sermon today was about faith," he would say, a bite of eggplant parmesan steaming on his fork. My father cooked on Sundays, which meant my mother's merciful early dismissal from the table was out of the question. "It was about how people should continue believing in God, even when evidence to the contrary is incredible." He would take the bite, chew, and swallow. "But there *is* incredible evidence to the contrary." He took the time to meet each of our eyes, eyebrows raised.

If dinnertime was my father's microcosm of a college classroom, my older sister Lauren, a freshman in high school then, could have majored, minored, and specialized in looking bored as hell. This was no concern to my father, who had long cultivated a thick skin when it came to blank-faced students.

Besides, he knew he could count on his youngest daughter. Unlike my sister, at twelve, I was still a sucker for my father's Devil's Advocate sessions for one reason above all others: already I knew I didn't belong at Wildwood Methodist. These talks around the dinner table helped me make sense of my own doubts.

"How can you reconcile the evil of today's world," he would continue, "where people die agonizing deaths from incurable diseases, where they starve, where they are murdered, with the idea of a God who is perfect? This is what we're taught, that God is perfect and all powerful. But if that's true, doesn't it mean God's also orchestrating the evil?"

"Maybe we don't understand it," I would say. "Evil, I mean. Maybe God has a different definition for evil than we have. Maybe we don't know that definition, or we can't understand it."

"Ah." He had hooked one. "You're thinking along the lines of the fifth-century theologian Augustine of Hippo. Augustine maintained that evil exists only as an absence of good. Ignorance is evil, but it's merely the absence of knowledge, which is good. Disease is the absence of health; callousness the absence of compassion. In this thinking, God cannot be held responsible for causing evil, since it is only an absence of good. But J. L. Mackie believed that evil was evidence that God does not exist at all."

I can't be sure of what compelled my father, Sunday after Sunday, to play devil's advocate to Reverend Findley's well-meaning sermons. Probably he was simply readying himself to teach, priming the tools of his trade, his voice, his ability to get a discussion going. Or maybe, by challenging Findley's message, his aim was to indirectly bolster our confidence in it, as he often ended with a philosophical theory supporting the sermon rather than contradicting it.

Years later I would learn that there was something deeper at work in those Devil's Advocate sessions: my father's own soured history with fundamentalist Christian culture. Popular in Texas and with some of our church friends, this Bible Belt approach seemed to proclaim, *God said it, I believe it, that settles it.*

It was this kind of thinking that had caused my father's own break with Christianity, a period that had lasted almost twenty years, and began shortly after he graduated from high school in 1967. My father was headed to Wheaton College, a private Christian institution near Chicago, but by then, reacting to the widespread antiwar, antiauthoritarian attitude of American youth, Wheaton had prohibited drinking, smoking, and other emblems of hippie culture. The college mandated that each student sign an agreement to abide by these rules before beginning classes.

My father wasted no time in breaking this agreement. He drank and smoked and read voraciously, and then he made the mistake of starting to talk to other students about Karl Marx. Finally free from his own parents' hardline Southern Baptist beliefs and military family structure, my father grew his hair long and switched his major from engineering to philosophy. When he announced this decision over Christmas, my grandfather got up and left the table. Mary Ruth buried her face in her hands and began sobbing.

Back at Wheaton, late into the following spring semester, a group of generals were scheduled to watch Wheaton's ROTC unit march around the football field in formation. My father seized upon the occasion to stage a single-man protest of the Vietnam War. Dressed in a white sheet splattered with red paint, he dashed onto the field and marched around with the unit as the band began to play.

Wheaton asked my father to leave.

Though he eventually made it back to graduate—he couldn't stand living at home while attending classes at Tulane, and he missed the rigorous philosophy faculty at his former institution—Mary Ruth's son was forever changed. From then on he spent as little time as possible with his own parents. He didn't go to church, and he rarely called home. When he had to go home for breaks he insisted on hitchhiking, refusing my grandmother's pleas to let her buy him bus tickets. If he became a quieter, more obedient student at Wheaton, it was only because he had become so focused on philosophy that little else mattered. And so he remained, for years to come.

Church friends of mine who attended our Sunday dinners often left pale and shocked. "We don't talk like that. Not at my house," a girlfriend once leaned in to whisper to me. I was clearing the table after our most recent Devil's Advocate session.

She was agitated, almost scared. "We don't talk like that, Natalie. Ever."

☾

THERE'S AN OLD Jewish witticism that goes two Jews, three opinions. To many Jews, as it was to my father, questioning indicates an active mind, which Judaism, in its long-standing support of literacy, education, and self-study, inherently embraces.

Evidence of doubt as a virtue abounds in Judaism. There is no hard-and-fast doctrine, for instance, about an afterlife. Some Jews believe in a type of heaven, others don't, and believing or not believing, in most branches of Judaism, doesn't make you more or less Jewish. Instead the search, the working out of details, the presence of conflicting cogent viewpoints, the discussion, the "wrestling with God" almost trumps the arrival at an answer. To many Jews, doubt is sacred.

Was it any wonder that for me, the idea of struggling with God, of celebrating doubt rather than stifling it, felt familiar? Doubt meant family. Doubt meant my house, Houston, Sunday evenings, going around and around with my father in Devil's Advocate.

A week before I finalized my conversion, my mom called. My parents had taken the news of my conversion about as well one could expect. Like Joe, they had half anticipated it, maybe even saw it coming. After I'd taken Rabbi Kleinman's class at the University of Houston, started to attend services, and made Jewish friends—none of which I hid from them—and after relocating for graduate school and finding a synagogue in Indiana, my parents could hardly act surprised at my supposed "announcement." They were supportive, proud even. Or so I thought.

That day my mother brought up my conversion and got straight to the point. "You know your father is hurting."

"What? No. About me becoming Jewish?"

As a graduate student I was becoming more like my father. It was a tendency I had despised as a teenager, noticing the similarities that kept cropping up in our characters. My father seemed so ill fit for our Texan suburbs, embarrassingly unapologetic about his bookishness, the old Mazda he drove to campus, his vegetarian leanings, and his insatiable appetite for intellectual banter.

Yet I was beginning to appreciate him far more. I had become an excellent student because of him, because for me there was nothing foreign about college. In a way it was as if I had been there my whole life, and it was why, out of everyone in my family with whom I had shared the news about my conversion, I had worried the least about my father's reaction.

"He won't show it, but he's having a hard time."

"No way. Dad?"

"You may not know this," my mom sighed. "But he only started attending church again after you girls were born."

This had never occurred to me. I went quiet. My father had returned to Christianity as a result of becoming a parent.

"He stayed away for a long time. Lord knows he wasn't attending when we met. Then you girls came along . . . I don't know. Even when he did go back, he couldn't help himself. Remember all those Sunday dinners?"

"Devil's Advocate."

"Devil's Advocate."

By then my father was in his fifth year as president of Alpena Community College. He was a far cry from the long-haired, antiestablishment twenty-something I had seen in pictures. After completing his own graduate work, he had been hired as a philosophy professor in the 1980s. He had met my mom and started a family. At work he had emerged as a leader in his faculty union. Those were the days of Devil's Advocate sessions at our house in Houston, but now, fifteen years later, states away, somehow my father had landed squarely on the other side. He wore a suit to work every day and kept his hair short. He watched the college's bottom line like a hawk. He called his parents every week and stayed on the phone for more than an hour.

How much of that slow transformation, a quarter-century in the making, I began to wonder, was the result of him returning to religion? To the very one he had fled as a young man? In becoming a good father, he had become a good son again.

Yet even as he made his way back into Christianity, he had toiled to create his own questioning version of it. One that wouldn't squelch deliberation but celebrate it. "Not sure I could even be counted as a Christian," my father once joked. "Jesus was a radical nomad. He said, 'Leave all your things and follow me.' But I would never leave your mom. If that's the way, the truth, and the life, I'm not for it." My father still stayed thirsty for an opposing viewpoint, and he still moved about the world like a much taller man, yet more and more, as he grew older, he seemed to be fighting against a former version of himself.

Was I that former version?

As my conversion drew closer this was something I thought about often. Is that why my father felt hurt? I had become unaffiliated, like he was in his youth, only I had taken it one step further. He had worked hard at making room in Christianity for people like me, for people like himself—for the doubters. Now I was never coming home. I never asked him about this. The hurting. If he was hurt, it was a wound my father repaired in private. He had said so little about my conversion I assumed he fully supported it, but now I knew that wasn't true.

In the months following my conversion my mother urged my father to reach out to the Jewish temple of Alpena, one I didn't know existed until my parents found it. A house among houses, Temple Beth-El stood in a quiet side street in Alpena, its single differentiating factor a small bronze plaque posted outside designating it a temple. Inside, the living room had been converted to a sanctuary, and behind the ark were the rabbi's quarters and a library.

In addition to their Sunday church services in Alpena, my parents started attending Temple Beth-El. This astonished me then as it does now. Temple Beth-El's congregation was too small to warrant the presence of a rabbi, but whenever the Jews of Alpena—a meager, aging crew, no doubt outliers themselves—arrived on Friday evenings to light candles, to celebrate Shabbat, and to enjoy a Seder meal together, Patricia and Olin Joynton joined them.

They brought hot dishes and questions. They exchanged contact information with members, and they learned the Hebrew prayers and songs. They even learned enough to follow along with services when they visited me, and my temple, near Purdue. They took book recommendations and read them, and when Joe was hired full time at the college and it was clear we would stay in Mason County, they asked me what I planned to do about the fact that there was no temple, and no Jews, in Ludington. All this not as potential members of the Jewish faith, but as parents.

☾

THOSE HEBREW PRAYERS and songs were a good part of what drew me to Judaism. The idea of speaking to God in a different language, a language separate from English, the vernacular I used for paying bills, listening to advertisements, scanning tabloids, filling out tax returns, tuning into workplace gossip, grabbing a drink with friends, and doing my real work of writing and teaching. In its own way Hebrew was magic, whisking me away from what Picasso called "the dust of everyday life."

What Hebrew was to me, math was to Joe. A great comfort, a challenge, an invitation, a creative refuge. A vessel through which scientific truths—the greatest truths, in his eyes—materialized.

It was a language he spoke and I didn't, or not in the same way. I could figure a 20 percent tip with no trouble, but it was hardly related to what Joe did teaching physics, these long equations interspersed with graphs. A rich amalgam of symbols, numbers, square roots, and run-on formulas. I had admired the whiteboards in his lab many times at the end of the day, the moment in an equation where one dry-erase marker ran out and another color took its place.

"If you die first," I asked one evening, "what do you want done with your body?" We were driving into Ludington for groceries. I can't remember how we stumbled into the subject, but it seemed as good a time as any to ask.

"I don't care. It's not like I'll be using it anymore."

"Do you think you would prefer burial or cremation?"

"Planning to poison my coffee after the wedding?"

I turned the heat up in the truck. "Maybe. But seriously, at some point, one of us is going to have to deal with this issue. I just want to know."

Joe kept his eyes on the road. Outside the window a field of pie pumpkins, the stouter cousins of the jack-o'-lantern kind, slid by in the October twilight.

"I guess you could donate my body to science."

I thought for a moment. "I can do that. Though that doesn't leave me anywhere to visit you." The road widened and we turned west onto the highway. "That's okay," I added then. "I'm sure we'll see each other again."

We stopped at a red light. "You know, I'm not so sure about that. Technically energy never ceases to exist. It only changes." Joe turned to face me. "But I think it's more of a lights-out situation."

☾

CONVERSATIONS LIKE THESE made it hard to believe Joe had spent the first decade of his schooling at St. Anne's of Alpena, the double-spired Catholic church where his older brothers had been taught by nuns and where the class sizes remained so small throughout his time there, he once told me, that even as his interest in girls amplified, he failed to see how any in his class were potential mates. "We had known each other from kindergarten," he said. "They seemed like family. For Christ's sake, our sex ed class was called 'New Creation.'"

Like so many, Joe had experienced a natural turning away from religion at the brink of adulthood, but it was his studies at college that cemented that change. Any return to faith seemed highly improbable for my future husband.

Despite being raised by a mother whose quiet devotion exemplified the best Catholicism had to offer, from her regular attendance at Mass to the strays she took in, Joe would not be following suit. He had stopped attending services at the earliest opportunity. He had never spoken with his mother about it, though he assured me that in his family such avoidance was normal.

That October as I ramped up efforts to email rabbis from around the state, hoping to find one who would wed a Jew and a non-Jew they had never met, the outlook looked bleaker than ever. Joe had offered to encourage my faith however I saw fit, but just as he would never return to Catholicism, he would never become Jewish.

One Sunday morning we were out for a walk in Ludington when we passed a couple in their mid-fifties dressed up and going to church. She held a Bible, he held her hand. Bundled up against the wind, they crossed into the parking lot of St. Bernard's. I watched them disappear inside.

"Do you ever think that we're missing something?" I asked. "You know, the family that prays together stays together, all that jazz."

"Nah." Then Joe smiled. He put his hand on my shoulder. "But Natalie, I'm glad you asked. I have been meaning to talk to you about the virtues of atheism."

I chuckled and elbowed him away. "I'm serious."

"I'm serious too. Those people? You don't know the first thing about those people. Maybe they pray together, but maybe they're awful roommates. Maybe she's a neat freak and he's a slob. Maybe they never have sex. Maybe he's got thousands of dollars' worth of debt from his Winnie the Pooh collector items."

I laughed out loud.

"Everyone is missing something," Joe said.

"This is a big something."

☾

I DECIDED NOT to press the conversion issue. My own past had made me allergic to the idea of proselytizing and beyond that, I knew Joe couldn't accept the idea of God. God was unprovable, and to scientifically minded people like Joe, this often meant that there were better explanations.

If a higher power existed at all for Joe, it was in those equations, in the curiosity sparked in his students, in the unintuitive nature of physics, in the movement of molecules, magnetic pulls, and the secrets of space. He would dislike that observation, as it annoyed him most when people tried to synthesize science and religion. When the Higgs boson was discovered and dubbed the "God particle" by the news media, Joe took it personally. "That's science journalism," he said, spotting me reading a press release. "It's not science."

"What's the difference?"

"The difference is that God has nothing to do with it. This is what happens when writers try to dress things up."

The part of me that was most like my father sat up and listened, ready for a debate.

"In an attempt to make science appealing to everyone, these reporters use riveting yet inexact language. They use clickbait headlines that generate further misunderstanding. Science does not need a makeover for the masses. It needs to be described in clear and careful terms."

"From what I gather the Higgs field serves as a type of universal backdrop that gives mass to otherwise massless particles," I told him, "effectively steering them toward possible futures as more complex entities. The discovery of Higgs boson confirms the existence of the entire field, right?"

"Yes. But that's not God."

"I could see how a writer could build a bridge between this reality and the idea of God," I argued. "What we're talking about here is an outside force giving mass to the otherwise massless."

Joe bristled then. "I can see how a writer could make that mistake too."

That October as we continued our search for a rabbi, even as I wished things were easier, I tried to keep something in mind. If Judaism was at my core, science was at Joe's, and it was not always the kind that coexisted peacefully with organized religion.

Yet each time I tried to imagine him otherwise, as an affiliated anything—Catholic or Jew—something about Joe fell apart in my mind. Joe reading the Torah, Joe saying the rosary—these images were doomed from the start, I reminded myself. That alternate Joe, the religious believer, was someone I did not recognize. That person I didn't know, and I didn't love.

Months earlier I had caught Joe on his knees between the maples in our front yard. It was still summer then, and he was facing the orchard, his head tilted forward and down. His back was toward me and at first glance, I thought there was something wrong with him, then realized this was because he seemed to be praying.

A stillness encircled his body, one that kept me from rushing over or calling out. Instead from the porch I craned my neck. Joe was clutching something. In his right hand was a thin blade of grass, and in the other, opened like a prayer book, was his plant-identification guide. He was holding the blade against the page, and the page against the light.

☾

IT WAS THE last Friday in October when Art Thigpen arrived, his truck bed stacked high with oak logs. Pushing seventy, lit cigarette drooping from his bottom lip, baseball cap pulled so low it nearly covered the wood seller's eyes, he brought with him what appeared to be two young men from the local juvenile detention center.

I had arrived back from teaching just in time to witness the spectacle. They pulled the truck around to the back of the farmhouse and stood at the edge of the tailgate, flinging log after log onto the concrete platform near the woodstove. There was something uneasy about the whole situation for me, how each log hit the ground, how after a while the boys didn't even bother to look where they were pitching and just let the logs fly and smack against the concrete, fly and smack. After ten minutes, two stacks of wood as tall as the truck itself were left. Art and his delinquents drove off.

I stood in the yard in my sweater dress, leggings, and leather boots. The wind was up and it looked like it was about to rain again.

Joe came out of the house. "You may want to change your clothes."

I turned away from him to mask my surprise. "Sure."

It hadn't occurred to me that Joe would ask for my help stacking wood. A few moments later I emerged in layered pajamas and the neon-orange beanie Joe had bought for the upcoming hunting season. I had found a pair of gardening gloves and slipped them over my hands as if there were any hope the thin cotton would prevent a splinter.

Then we stacked wood. And we stacked wood. For hours. Log after log, I carried an armful over to Joe, who heaved it the other half of the way into the shed, hoisting each log into its place in a neat column.

"Like Tetris," he said. We weren't half done with the first cord but already it seemed as if a whole day had passed. In the October chill our hot breath lingered.

Mostly I managed to make it back to Joe, my arms full of wood, before he came out for more. I was proud of this but I had been picking the lighter logs. Branches, really. Then there were no more branches. Late afternoon had sunk into evening and I scanned the huge pile still left for us to stack. I summoned all my strength to haul a thicker piece, undoubtedly some trunk slice, from the concrete. I moaned.

"Warms you twice," Joe called over his shoulder.

I moaned again. I was no longer cold. My arms felt lit from within. As I lumbered over hauling my trunk slice, I was simultaneously livid and grateful Joe was not moving to help me. This, I suddenly realized, was a test. If Joe was missing the Jewish component, I was missing something sacred to him as well—a willingness to live and work at the edge of the woods.

By the time we finished stacking the first cord it was nightfall. My arms felt as if they would fall off. We were bathed in wood dust. Beyond the shed Joe opened the stove and placed the top three logs from the first column inside. It occurred to me that until that night, not only had I never stacked wood, I also had no idea how to start a fire. Joe balled up old newspapers and placed them under the logs, and I watched him set the match.

It was not how I'd been hoping to spend the beginning of the weekend. But as the heat from the stove filled the farmhouse, I discovered I wasn't as tired as I'd thought. We toasted and buttered some bread, shared a beer, and heated up some potato soup. We ate in silence but then found ourselves in the bedroom, reveling in how comfortable the house had suddenly become, our sheets no longer freezing but inviting. Joe rested on the edge of the bed then pulled me close. I buried my face in his hair.

9

THE ELDER

In November I spent my mornings waiting for first light. Sitting in the kitchen in my running gear, hat, and gloves, eating a banana and checking the window, I was slightly alarmed at the rate at which the days were shortening in Michigan. The previous summer's 7 a.m. sunrises and 10 p.m. sunsets seemed like a hiccup of memory. Could this really be the same place? I kept thinking, taking another bite, my body restless for the road.

I knew runners who would go at any time of day, including at night, but they lived back in Houston and ran in the wealthier neighborhoods of River Oaks or West U. In Mason County, Michigan, everything in my gut told me to wait until full morning. Outside the dawn moved like a slow pink curtain over the hardwoods.

This waiting instinct had something to do with my urban past, but I knew it had more to do with the general eeriness of late autumn in the country, with the bare swaths of woods hunching over the road, and with the long spaces between farmhouses, and the empty harvested fields, now cut to stubble.

It was that and the fact that drivers took the roads surrounding Replica Dodge extremely slow. Often it ended up being just me and some truck, the vehicle disappearing from view down one hill and then emerging at the crest of another, closer hill. This approach always felt menacing, like something out of a horror film—the driver's face obscured by the windshield, the woods framing us both. Now that we had been at Replica Dodge a full season, I knew which vehicles belonged to our few neighbors and which were strangers, and whenever I was out running and a truck I didn't recognize turned down the road, I was always reminded of Flannery O'Connor's Misfit. *No pleasure but meanness.*

Once a truck slowed to a stop beside me. Thankfully, I was in front of one of the farmhouses rather than a lonely stretch of woods, but I didn't recognize it as belonging to anyone in our area. I turned to face the vehicle as the man inside rolled down his window. He had blond hair and wore sunglasses. "Should be calling you for scout reports," he said, flicking cigarette ash onto the dirt near my shoes.

Scout reports? What was he talking about? Out of the corner of my eye I tried to gauge whether there were cars parked in the driveway of the nearby farmhouse. "I have no idea what you're referencing."

"Deer season. Coming soon. Seen any bucks?"

My friends in Mason County kept insisting that I was safer running these hills than I would be in any city, with dozens of vehicles roaring past me per minute. The statistics were far in my favor here, they reassured me, but I had remained less than convinced because something about there being lots of people around—even some of the wrong kind—seemed safer than these wooded hills and the occasional stranger. I needed daylight between me and those slow trucks. I needed pepper spray, I decided, and a big dog.

The latter I had. Scruggs had come into our lives three months prior in the capacity of my running companion. He was a blue heeler, his wiry hair a mix of black, gray, and tan whorls, but there was another breed in him that made him significantly larger than his purebred cattle-chasing cousins. On the day we visited the shelter, Scruggs, sixty pounds and sporting a coyote's smirk, sat calmly in his kennel as the other dogs howled.

So far he'd proved to be the perfect dog. He responded to directions, looked mean but wasn't, didn't pee indoors, and took to Replica Dodge as if he had lived there his whole young life. During the warmer months he had chased woodchucks from the Lady's Emporium deep into the surrounding woods, but by November it was so cold he needed additional motivation to go outside. Having me as his companion provided it. That morning, like all the others recently, he was waiting with me in the kitchen.

Opening day of deer season, or simply Opening Day, as it's called in Mason County, was treated like a local holiday. This I had learned the week before. That Thursday only a handful of students had arrived to my morning composition class. Halfway through our first assignment description I stopped. "Where are your peers?"

One student stared at me. Another lifted her book to hide her grin.

"Hunting," a third offered.

"Wow," said a fourth. "You really are new here."

As a joke in the days that followed, my students brought in pictures taken with their cell phones to show me after class. Images of them crouching over their "kills," holding some buck's head upright by its antlers so that it too, bloody-mouthed and glass-eyed, faced the camera. These photos reminded me that even my most subdued students had other sides to them. I winced but did my best to convey congratulations.

Maybe that's why they brought them in, to watch me squirm and try to save face. Either way I couldn't wrap my head around this practice of cataloguing one's "kills" as if human beings were still the hopeful underdogs of the planet, not the other way around. Why take pictures or hang stuffed heads over fireplaces? Why did we need more confirmation of our place in the food chain? Wasn't this practice the equivalent of a conqueror's brag? Besides, the little I knew about guns and scopes made me skeptical of the supposed skill it took to shoot an animal.

Yet this, I reminded myself, was only further evidence of my own background, of my urban family who had maintained a mostly vegetarian diet, serving dishes like African brown nut stew, stuffed bell peppers, and meat-free lasagna for dinner. We had never hunted or fished. We never owned a gun.

Once when I was six or seven, on vacation in Hot Springs, I had fed the catfish in my grandparents' pond for five days straight until on the sixth—for reasons I don't recall—I reached in, snatched one out, and flung it onto the grass. The fish writhed and flailed and kept opening its ugly mouth, and then after a moment it fell still, nothing but the gills fanning and closing. I panicked, pitched the fish back in the water, ran inside the house, washed my hands, and never told anyone what I had done.

At last, light streamed through the window and I pulled on my neon-orange beanie—a signal to hunters I wasn't a deer—leashed the dog, and we were off. There was a week of firearm hunting season left, and along our route that morning I counted the deer blinds. I wondered how many hunters were inside those small, shack-like structures placed in the middle of fields or against the woods. Eventually I counted more blinds than farmhouses. Maybe some hunters had already gone home with the dawn, but still others were lying in wait, I imagined, watching for that buck to step into the clearing and hoping for a clean shot. Occasionally I heard them, those shots, a crack of sound that always seemed far off.

The only people I knew in Texas who hunted went to ranches teeming with ten-point bucks, so the first time I saw a deer blind was on an afternoon drive I took with my parents shortly after they had moved to Alpena. I was eighteen and I initially assumed that the blinds were outhouses. I couldn't figure out why their owners had built them so far from their homes. Poor kids, I remember thinking, no flushable toilets, and a long walk in the dark.

Suddenly Scruggs surged forward, tugging hard on his leash. I struggled to catch my footing, then stopped to scold him, but his eyes were locked on something in the field west of us. In the weak light I squinted too until I could see it: an animal zigzagging through the alfalfa. It was a good distance away, but I could see the run wasn't a typical gait. The animal was loping, dashing, sprinting forward in a mad blur. At first I couldn't quite make it out but finally I recognized it as a deer. Of course, I thought, letting go of my breath. A deer. I bent down beside the dog. Ears erect, eyes still locked, he whimpered as we watched the zigzagging animal. Then all of a sudden, in its full haul across the field, it fell flat.

It was as if someone had jerked it down by its neck. Was it hurt? I considered walking over, combing through the alfalfa to check on the wounded animal, then realized how stupid this would be during hunting season. The dog lowered his head and sniffed the dirt, whatever scent he had seized upon now lost. But I kept my eyes on the field, unsure of what to do next.

A hunter emerged from the far woods beyond the field. He wore a neon-orange vest, the same color as the beanie I wore on my head, and I watched as he walked, studying the earth as if it were a map. He was tracing the animal's tracks. Or the blood trail. The hunter came to the patch of field where the deer had fallen, set down his gun, kneeled, and drew something from his side. The broad knife gleamed in the light, reflecting the sunrise, and I turned away as he made the first cut.

☾

ALONG ONE OF my typical running routes on the dirt roads, there stood a nameless white building. Located less than a mile from Replica Dodge, it looked like some kind of small community hall or church. It was bigger than a house, but not by much, and it had broad double doors. Its gravel parking lot was hemmed by maple and beech trees, now bare in the cold, and a rawboned gully skirted under the road north of the building. I had passed it a hundred times, but I'd never seen anyone there. A few dawns after encountering the hunter, I decided to look inside.

Wiping the fog from a window and then cupping my hands around my eyes, I peered inside to see a basement full of banquet tables. Mission-style, stacked one on top of another, they were crafted of an exquisite blond wood. Was it birch? Poplar? I counted them. There were eight that I could see, and maybe more that I couldn't.

Since we had agreed to host our wedding reception in the barn, there had been a persistent image nagging at me. It wasn't the work involved—the massive labor to clean and renovate the space, which still awaited us—but rather one prompted by a recent conversation with a friend. I kept seeing our guests flying into Chicago, then driving four hours north to reach us. I imagined my family from Houston and friends from Santa Fe, Seattle, and New York. These attorneys, professors, architects, business owners. What would they think of Replica Dodge?

Then there was the issue of the event itself. Weddings were weighty affairs to begin with, but now more than ever they aimed at celebrating the uniqueness of each love story. From the save-the-date to the linens to the lighting, each detail had to make an idiosyncratic statement. Talk about pressure. Each reading, each song had to be some individual affirmation of the leap of faith Joe and I were about to take.

Or at least that's the version I had bought into because, cheesy as it sounded, I wanted that wedding, a once-in-a-lifetime party that represented both of us. Only so far we had no rabbi. Not a single teacher of my faith to stand up and say, *Here is a Jewish bride, here is the love of her life.* We had decided to host our wedding at home, only this place, I kept thinking, was not my home.

I had struggled with that sense of alienation from the moment I had arrived: the slow pace, the strange local rites of passage like Opening Day. I had killed my best friend's chickens because I didn't know to close a barn door at night. Exactly how could this wedding, I kept thinking—let alone this life—set deep in the Michigan woods, with no rabbi, no congregation, and no community, represent my half of the story?

Upon receiving a wedding invitation, an old friend from Houston had called me up. "What are you now," she teased, "some kind of Michigan hillbilly?"

That had been the breaking point. With her words banging in my brain, by late November I was on a mission. I would find a rabbi if it killed me. And even if our wedding was set in the Michigan woods, there were other details I could control. They were the smaller ones, admittedly, but in a fit bordering on panic, I wasted no time zeroing in on them. Flowers, guest book, favors. I spent hours online scanning options, visiting local vendors, poring over potential menus. And now here in front of me, in the basement of the white building, were eight blond tables that would fit perfectly in our renovated barn.

On the following Sunday I invited Jen over to run. When we came to the white building I convinced her to peer into the basement windows with me.

"Those are gorgeous," Jen agreed, turning back to the road and picking up speed. "You know who makes tables like that? Probably the same people who own that building."

"Who's that?" I said, stealing one more glimpse.

Jen raised her voice above the wind. "The Mennonites."

"The who?"

"You know—the ones who dress like the Amish, except in color."

☾

PROMISED LAND BAKERY, where Jen recommended I inquire further about the tables, was a small family-run business situated two miles south of Replica Dodge, even deeper into the country. The bakery was not unlike the nameless white building, only painted brown, and I arrived alone on a Tuesday afternoon. A bell jingled when I pushed the door open, and though I was the only customer, the three women working behind the counter didn't acknowledge my presence. Pretending to survey sourdough loaves, out of the corner of my eye I studied them, fetching ingredients, kneading dough, and bagging bread.

Their long dresses in simple patterns of purple and green seemed to swish as they moved about the bakery. They wore their hair pulled back and covered under something that looked like a small bonnet pinned at the back of the head, and their round faces were free of cosmetics. The shop was warm, heated by the ovens. A woven basket containing a few dollar bills sat on the counter near a simple cash register. Not realizing until later that Promised Land Bakery was a self-serve operation, I loitered around the shop until it became obvious I needed help.

Finally the oldest woman came over, looking a little exasperated. She wiped her hands on her apron. "Can I help you?" Her voice had a quick lilt. She sounded like no one else in Mason County I'd met. She crossed her arms.

"Yes," I placed an onion cheese loaf on the counter between us and pulled out my wallet. "Do you know who owns the white building out toward Chalmers? It looks like a church of some type, except there's no sign."

"The German Baptists." The woman handed me change for a five.

"The German Baptists?"

"A congregation elder owns the market off the highway."

She gave me a quick smile but there was something vacant about her gaze. It seemed as if she were staring through my body to some point at the opposite end of the bakery. Then I realized she was staring at the Star of David pendant on my necklace. The conversation was over.

"Thank you," I said and left.

☾

THE GERMAN BAPTISTS were not Amish or Mennonite, but I could see why Jen had made the association. From an outsider's perspective, all indicators of a conservative Christian sect were present: old-fashioned dress and large families. Small businesses that offered the basics, handmade chairs and tables, breads and sweets, all sold at arm's length to anyone immersed in the digital age. The German Baptist market, my final destination for finding out about the availability of those banquet tables, sat six miles east of Ludington. Even though it was situated right off the highway rather than deep in the countryside, I recognized the market immediately based on the similarity it shared with the other two modest structures I had visited. A sign outside read, "Bulk goods: sale on cheddar." I parked my car, buttoned my coat up to the neck, and opened the door.

The market was nearly empty. A man in his early fifties rifled through a basket of oranges, a woman with a baby scanned the dish soap options. The draft had found its way through a crack in the door and the market's concrete floor gave little insulation, and once more I found myself loitering about, unsure of what to say or do, or if I would recognize a congregation elder if one appeared.

It was in the crafts aisle that I came across something I didn't expect. "Huh," I said aloud, running my fingers over a small blue box of Hanukkah candles.

What an odd find, though timely, as Hanukkah was coming up in December. I imagined the sad sight of me lighting the menorah candles alone in Replica Dodge, but another thought buoyed me up. Hanukkah candles. In the German Baptist market. This could be a good sign. I picked up the box and placed it in my basket just as a bearded man came out from the back of the store rolling a dolly. He was older than my father and sported a wide-brimmed brown hat, suspenders, and a dark vest over his periwinkle button-up. Was this the elder? He looked like one.

I readied myself for another awkward exchange and headed to the cash register.

The man scanned the Hanukkah candles. His broad face bore deep lines at the brow.

"I've never seen these sold anywhere else around here," I said.

"Are you Jewish?" The elder asked, not looking up.

"Yes." I handed him a ten.

"Ah." The register zinged open. "The Bible teaches us that if we bless Israel, we too are blessed." His voice was stern, distant. The elder placed the Hanukkah candles in a plastic bag and held it out to me.

Oh, I thought, it's over. Already the brief transaction was ending and I had missed my chance. I took the bag from him and turned to go. Then I stopped. Your half of the story, I reminded myself.

"Do you own the white building off Chalmers?"

The elder looked up and, for the first time, straight at me.

"No. The congregation does." He crossed his arms like the woman in the bakery. "Why do you ask?" I sucked in another breath and launched into it. "I'm not from around here. My fiancé and I recently bought a house in the country, and we're hosting our wedding there next June, actually in the barn, or at least part of it—the reception—only right now it's stuffed full of a shitload of trinkets."

God. I had said *shitload* to the elder. Wonderful, I thought, real classy, now there was nothing to do but keep going. I described the country runs I took with the dog, how we had passed the white building a hundred times before I'd first peered inside its basement windows, how sorry I was for trespassing but, "Long story long," I declared, careening toward some semblance of an end, "I'm hoping to rent those tables for my wedding."

By now the elder was leaning against the back of the register, his face unreadable. "Sounds nice." He shrugged. "But I can't rent you those tables."

My face got hot. The young woman with the baby, who was crying now, came up to the register. There was nothing to do but leave.

"What I can do," the elder went on, "is allow you to petition the congregation."

"What?" I raised my voice over the crying baby.

"Services are Saturday mornings in that white building,"

That explained why I'd never seen cars there. I didn't run on Saturdays.

The elder smiled to reveal a mouth full of pristine white teeth. "Come, and bring your fiancé to plead your cause."

Outside in my car, I sat for a long time before starting it up. I repeated the elder's words about blessing Israel to myself, as if saying them would loosen some lost trivia buried in the back of my mind, but the German Baptists had not been covered in the World Religions course I had taken at the University of Houston.

Plead my cause? What did I know of these people? That they liked Jews, but maybe only because their Bible instructed them to "bless Israel"? Give me a break. How much were the banquet tables really worth? The day was bright but cold. I turned the key over, the radio down, the heat up. Pulling away from the market back onto the highway, I began to weigh the elder's odd offer.

Bring your fiancé to plead your cause. What century was this? I tried to imagine Joe in front of the German Baptists, rallying for the banquet tables that he couldn't care less about, and it was then I remembered something he had once confessed to me, years earlier. "As a boy," he said, "I always wanted to holler during Mass."

Maybe this was his chance.

☾

IN GETTING READY for the service, I deliberated about pinning back my hair. Covering it, making it look like what I could only guess was hidden beneath the women's head coverings at Promised Land Bakery. But I had never covered my head before, and the idea of doing it for the sake of eight banquet tables struck me as ridiculous. The whole situation now struck me as ridiculous.

Was I on this mission for the right reasons? Was this me claiming my wedding, my life—my half of the story—or was I doing this all just to prove to my urban friends and family that I hadn't become the punch line of that eternal joke city people tell about those who live in the country? That they're inferior? That they're rednecks, white trash, inbred hillbillies? Either way, I now had the distinct sense I was at the middle point of some saga that could not be abandoned. From my closet I chose black pants and a large sweater that hung rather than hugged.

All morning Joe huffed about the house. In a last-ditch effort to gauge our impending audience, he had read a Wikipedia article on German Baptists, only to discover that there were a dozen or so divisions: *German Baptist,* he reported, was a loose term, and we had no way of knowing whether this congregation was of the Old Order, the Conservative Grace Brethren, the Dunkards, or the New Dunkers.

What's more, at least one branch of the denomination didn't condone drinking or dancing. "And we're going to ask them to use their tables. For a wedding reception. With a DJ and hard liquor," he said, climbing into the truck.

Suddenly I felt the heat rise in my chest. "Having the reception in the barn was your idea," I shot back. "I'm just trying to make it a little more my own. I love those tables."

"There are perfectly good tables for rent in Ludington."

"So? You know what one of my students told me last week? That at her wedding they filled a kiddie pool with ice to keep the cans of beer cold. Is that what you want, Joe? No rabbi and a kiddie pool filled with ice and canned beer?"

"Wait. How is it my fault you can't find a rabbi to officiate our wedding? That's your faith, not mine."

"Yeah, you know, for a moment there, I forgot I was a Jew." At some point I had started shouting. Joe hit the brakes and pulled over. He cut off the engine and we became quiet, watching a pair of crows pick over a cornfield.

"Natalie. What is happening?"

I waved my hand toward the windshield in a broad gesture to indicate our surroundings. "This is happening, Joe. This place. If I had a temple I wouldn't need a rabbi at our wedding. But I keep trying to find my footing here and I can't. Spiritually, culturally, anything. I can't. Doesn't that matter to you?"

For a long moment Joe didn't say anything. I could see him try-ing to figure out how best to respond, but coming up short. Finally he pulled back onto the road.

"We have a lot to be thankful for here," he began. "We have a good job—"

"No. This may be your happy ending." I shook my head. "But it's not mine."

☾

A FEW MILES later when we arrived at the white building, a woman washing mud off her boots at the outdoor pump waved us over. "Welcome." She hurried over. "I'm Donna."

We introduced ourselves to Donna. Then to Glen and Rhonda. Then to Mary and Noah. Then to Isaac and Ruth and their children, Matthew, Clay, and Hannah. For the next thirty minutes, we introduced ourselves over and over as members of the congregation arrived, parked their family vans or trucks, and approached us with the same brand of beaming curiosity. The elder, seeing the swarm around us at the door, tipped his hat and went inside, and by the time we made it to the back pew, we had met nearly everyone in the small congregation. They smiled at us, they shook our hands. Clearly they had been expecting our visit.

Inside the white building was a single room, and in the middle of it was a woodstove warming those coming in from the cold. The building's dark hardwood floors were a fitting complement to the white walls and tall windows. There were sixteen wooden pews, eight on each side. No sacred art. No crosses. It was obvious that men and women sat on separate sides of the aisle, but Donna insisted that Joe and I sit together. The older women like Donna sat closer to the front of the building, while young girls in patterned dresses filed into the row in front of us, conveniently across the aisle from the unmarried men's pew. Glances were exchanged.

The fight we had just experienced was typical of us. They were few and far between, given our appreciation of debate, but when real fights happened they were quick and painful, and always ended with each of us retreating into distinct grand silences. These silences guaranteed we would avoid saying anything we could not unsay. Sometimes those silences lasted for hours, sometimes for days.

I watched as four men, including the one from the market, stationed themselves at the tables at the front of the room. Elders, I realized. Plural.

The service began with a hymn sung from a book that seemed pulled from Replica Dodge's own church, a handheld leather volume with tiny bold black print. No instruments accompanied the singing. The collective voice of the small congregation was austere and fetching. The song was simple enough but I didn't sing along. When I glanced up, I wasn't surprised to find that Joe's lips were also closed.

Then the hymn ended and, all at once, everyone in the congregation turned to face us.

The German Baptists took to their knees. We wouldn't sing, but there was no way Joe and I could remain sitting as the congregation prayed, kneeling, facing our direction at the very back of the room. I shot a look at Joe, who mouthed *I don't know* and began bending down.

Perhaps for him, after years of attending Mass, this was not especially bizarre. As an elder struck up a prayer, I too knelt. I looked at my hands, clasped in a way they never were when I prayed in Hebrew, with my eyes open and my arms at my side. We were so low to the ground I could count the mouse droppings near the double doors.

"My heart is fixed, O God, my heart is fixed," the elder said. This was the verse that was the subject of the day's sermon, and for the next half hour, the congregation was reminded of "Satan's real work in the world" and the power of "good intentions matched by right action." The sermon was given by the youngest of the four elders. Afterward, as he sat down, another elder rose to take his place.

Oh, God, I thought. That was only the first.

I looked again at Joe, who had such an exasperated look on his face I wasn't sure he would stay. Clearly I had landed him in the seventh circle of hell. The rest of the morning dribbled by as we discovered that not only would each elder speak, each succeeding one would speak for longer than the previous elder. For four hours we sat in the sermon hall. Inside the stove, the fire roared. Morning became afternoon, and during the final hour-long sermon rendered by the eldest elder, I kept touching Joe's knee, hoping he wasn't asleep.

In their row ahead, the young unmarried women were taking notes on each elder's message. In little notebooks they underlined words like *confidence* and *light,* copied from Bible verses and bits of hymn. All of them were doing this except for one, whom I watched with increasing fascination. Her back was toward me and I couldn't remember her face from the introductions earlier. Her head cloth, like all of the other coming-of-age daughters, was pinned neatly in place, but this girl was not taking pious notes. She was sketching. First a face: half-smiling lips, then an eye. A slender neck next and arms like willow limbs, then the full curve of a breast. She finished by drawing a tight gown on the woman's body that was nothing like the conservative dress she was wearing.

Having no idea when we'd be asked to plead our cause, I kept waiting for a signal. It never came, and the German Baptist service ended with a final prayer. Had we missed our cue? But then Donna was ushering us downstairs to the basement, to the very room whose windows I had peered into many mornings before, where the exquisite blond tables hosted a parade of food: egg salad, sweet rice with raisins, steaming barley soup, beef casserole, buttered croissants, molasses cookies, a tower of fresh-cut fudge. My stomach ballooned at the sight. After everyone had gathered downstairs and the children had washed their hands, the eldest elder stepped forward.

"You all have noticed these two this morning," he said, pointing in our direction. The basement went from quiet to silent. Here we go, I thought. "This woman's fiancé is here to plead her cause."

Joe stepped to the center of the crowd of German Baptists. He had his hands buried in his pockets but he stood erect, his shoulders back. He looked confident. He stood meeting the eyes of the women and men equally.

"Good morning," he said. "My name is Joe, and this is my fiancée Natalie. We recently moved into Bill Broadwell's farmhouse, the one with the little city out front." He went on to describe how we had decided to host our wedding at home, and how I had come to peer in the church windows on my daily runs. A few congregants grinned.

"These tables are a perfect fit for our reception. They are strong and beautiful and well built."

What shocked me was that there was no edge in Joe's voice. Despite our fight, despite huffing around the house all morning, despite having spent the last four hours in church—the last place he wanted to be—he didn't seem the least bit angry. I was reminded of why I had fallen hard for him. Joe could seamlessly shift from the ultimate curmudgeon to the most charming man in the room, and now, even if he was faking it, he was doing it for me.

"In the spirit of full disclosure," he said in ending the plea, "ours will be a Jewish ceremony." Then he looked right at me. "There will be a rabbi. And drinking and dancing."

No one flinched. When Joe concluded his petition a few seconds later, one of the elders bowed his head in prayer.

Though the German Baptists wouldn't give us an answer that day, preferring to discuss it privately among themselves, something happened as we started to eat. I saw the tables close up for the first time. They were just as exquisite as I had hoped, made of a high-gloss golden wood marbled with dark knots, but it was then I realized I no longer cared about them.

In the Babylonian Talmud it's written that forty days before a child is born, its mate is determined. On the bench I found Joe's hand and laced it with mine. In a way, this was like having a fixed heart.

I blew across my spoonful of barley soup. I wanted to say something, to apologize or rationalize, but then the elder from the market came over and sat down beside us, and soon our table was filling up on both sides with German Baptists, eating, laughing, engaging each other, even flirting, at once transformed from austerity to vibrancy.

10

BREAKING UP WITH CHRISTMAS

IN REPLICA DODGE the first snow fell. The ground was covered. Snow collected on the roofs of the church, barbershop, and general store, and as much as I had dreaded winter in Michigan, as I watched those first flakes glide down, the girl in me leapt at the sight. All those Decembers in Houston wishing for snow, and now here it was, right on time.

The wind was like a gentle wave over the hills, ushering down the white at a soft angle. The snowfall muted Replica Dodge's standard chorus of bird song and cow bellows from the farm down the road, but it wasn't as if the world became silent. In a way the blanket of snow made the occasional sound seem even louder: the whine of the woodstove door as Joe opened it, the hiss of a newspaper catching fire from orange-black ash. Unlike in Houston, December in Michigan looked the part.

Winter in southeast Texas was a wild range of thirty-degree dawns and eighty-degree afternoons. When I was growing up, the single coat I had forgotten about all year would reappear in my closet each December as if drawn up from the bottom of some deep well. Lauren and I were bundled up at the bus stop in the morning, but by the time school ended, it was not unusual for us to sweat in our pullovers. My father's habanero peppers grew slower but still ripened.

Texas winters were a surreal mix of peppermint mochas and sunshine, of fake frost scrawled in washable paint on library windows. White lights were strung up to bathe the green lawns of our subdivision. Rainstorms threatened to become hailstorms, and anytime they did, every stone pelting the trunk of our family Lincoln seemed to promise something far more magical: real snow.

Real snow was rare in Houston and never arrived on Christmas, but as a girl that didn't keep me from wishing for it. It was a wish annually rekindled the day after Thanksgiving, when I would go headlong into my fanfare, begging my parents to haul down our decorations from the attic, those handmade ornaments from Sunday school, our glass nativity scene with its missing shepherd, the front door wreath we displayed year after year, even as its red berries chipped to reveal the Styrofoam beneath. There were crumpled bows, plastic candy canes, and our family's faux velvet stockings. There were Christmas CDs cranked to play at maximum volume, "Feliz Navidad" blaring as my parents dragged that Holy Grail of holiday cheer down the hall once more.

Our Big Fake Christmas Tree was at least twenty years old, having been passed down from my mother's mother to our family before I was born, and each year it returned to its sunlit space near the couch a little more bedraggled than the year before. Its limbs were splayed, bent back as if broken, but each year we would work out its kinks. It was a Joynton family tradition, straightening the Big Fake Christmas Tree, and then topping it with its longtime partner, an angel straight out of the 1970s we called Disco Queen. Her bleached afro was teased high, her blue eye shadow electric.

Later I would realize that the recycled tree and angel, along with the rest of our dilapidated decorations, were a testament to my parents' total aversion to the mania surrounding the holiday season in Houston. This citywide mania—much like my own— emerged the day after Thanksgiving and was seemingly fueled by a collective and acute awareness of the single thing our southern landscape would never give us: a white Christmas.

Instead Houstonians hunted that feeling down for purchase. That quaint-country-house-nestled-atop-a-snowy-hill feeling, that smoke-chuffing-from-the-chimney feeling, the saddled horses and wooden sleds, the cold, the coming in from the cold—all of it was attainable, my city and I seemed to believe, with an expensive visit to Home Depot's garland aisle. And with regular excursions to one of the city's malls, where some North Pole Village, with its profes- sional gift wrapping, whirring snow machine, and perfectly pink- cheeked Santa Claus, helped us all forget the seventy-degree weather right outside.

My mother wasn't buying it. Neither was my father. They were too bookish, too liberal, too grown up. When I was eleven or twelve years old, I remember wondering if our Christmas decora- tions would even make it down from the attic without my annual day-after-Thanksgiving pomp and circumstance, because no one in our immediate family—not even Lauren, at a mere two years older than I—seemed to catch the season as soon as it arrived.

No one coveted its clichés as I did, the cardboard Advent calendars with their hidden chocolates, the iced sugar cookies and wish-list making, the transformation of JCPenney's and Dillard's into palaces of green and red. That same year, my mother came into my bedroom. It was the middle of December and right before my bedtime. In her hand was a pillowcase, lumpy from whatever she had stuffed inside. She had been working long hours and her face was a brilliant streak of fatigue and stress. "These are your sister's gifts." She held the pillowcase out to me. "Can you wrap them?"

A moment later I heard her knock at my sister's door down the hall.

If my parents hoped their ambivalence toward the holiday would serve as a cue for me, year after year I missed that cue. More likely, when it came to Christmas in Houston, my parents remained a blip on the radar of my greater environment. Unlike my peers', my appetite for the holiday kept growing well into my teens, as the simpler pleasures my parents championed became just as succulent to me as the holiday's purchasable treats.

I loved the moment each night when we would plug in our lights, that lone string of color flickering to outline our porch. Or the final day of school before break, when in the bustle between classes I would find my best friend to exchange presents. Then— free at last—the anticipation of the countdown to the arrival of relatives: uncles and aunts and cousins, my sister at the piano, perfecting "O Little Town of Bethlehem" for my grandparents. Then the sleeping four to a room and waking too early, too revved up to sleep again, and the long wait for cheese grits and bacon, sticky buns and coffee. Even in snowless, sunny Houston, as a girl it was all worthy, delicious, and equal, each Christmas a feast for spiritual scavengers like me.

Seasonal preparations at Wildwood Methodist were no exception. Lauren and I were members of the church's youth choir, the group annually charged with the task of re-creating the nativity onstage for the Christmas Eve service. The year I played a shepherd we were told, at the last minute, that we would be incorporating real farm animals into our performance. When the bumble of livestock showed up an hour before we were set to go onstage, the church was a bedlam of costume changes and set repairs, and this is probably why I missed the farmer's single direction to that room full of city kids: the sheep follow the goats. *Not* the other way around.

An hour later, in my shepherd's robe and cotton beard, I made my grand entrance. The sanctuary was full and I charged up the center aisle, but from the second I stepped forward, my woolly partner did not. The sheep stood staring back at me blankly. I tugged on the rope again—hard. Then the sheep began bleating. It dug its hooves into the church tile, then crapped on the floor. The youth choir was doling out a solemn "O Come, O Come, Emmanuel" as I pulled, shoved, and negotiated my woolly partner up to Mary and Joseph onstage. (And was there ever a better analogy than this? Tugging, shoving, and negotiating to reach Jesus's side?) Eventually I wrangled the sheep up to the manger, though by then I was sweating profusely.

After the performance we changed clothes and joined our parents in the pews. White candles with cardboard sleeves were passed around, someone lowered the lights, and the sanctuary faded from dim to dark. Then the first candle was lit, then its flame shared with a neighbor, and so on until the light spread in rows, transforming our congregation into a sea of warm faces singing in the dark.

There was a girl who had a voice like a bell and it rang out above us. *In the bleak midwinter / Frosty wind made moan / Earth stood hard as iron / Water like a stone.* At twelve, I thought it was the most beautiful song I'd ever heard. *Snow had fallen, snow on snow / Snow on snow.* I listened and thought I would weep.

This was always the sum total of Christmas Eve at Wildwood Methodist. It produced in me a sudden and sweeping affection for a faith that otherwise, for the rest of the year, felt foreign. But somehow this service managed to dominate my doubts, and so for a few moments on December 24 each year, I truly belonged in the pew next to my parents.

I clung to those moments of belonging. As if they could explain away the other fifty Sundays a year when it was clear that Christianity was no home for me. The Christmas Eve service at Wildwood gave me hope that I could be a Christian—someday—that if given enough time, I could come around to Jesus and avoid hell.

Another small beacon of hope was my first name, Natalie. My parents had named me for the actress Natalie Wood, but once, right around Christmas, Mary Ruth had taken me aside to reveal my name's original meaning. We were spending the holidays in Arkansas that year, having traveled the eight hours from Houston to my grandparents' house in Hot Springs. There were sugared yams in the oven and corn on the cob boiling on the stove, and we had just returned from church. I was heading downstairs when Mary Ruth pulled me close in a sudden embrace that was almost unheard of for my grandmother. The amethyst pendant on her necklace pained my cheek, but Mary Ruth smelled of lemon rinds and Fels-Naptha laundry soap. Her hands were warm around my waist and I breathed her in.

"Natalie Ruth," she whispered, then released me to brush down the pleats of my dress. Her formal tone took back over. "Natalie." Mary Ruth looked me in the eye. "From the Latin *natale domini*. Your name means Christmas Day."

☾

THE ANNUAL JEWISH calendar includes over twenty holidays. As a practicing Jew, this means I never have to wait long for the next festival or solemn commemoration. There is Simchat Torah, day of celebrating Torah. There is Tisha B'Av, which commemorates the destruction of the temples in Jerusalem. There is Sukkot, Feast of Tabernacles, and Tu BiShvat, New Year of the Trees. There is Yom HaShoah, *shoah* meaning catastrophe, the time each year when we memorialize the 6 million Jews lost in the Holocaust.

Contrary to popular thought, Hanukkah is not "Christmas for the Jews." Hanukkah commemorates the successful outcome of a military revolt led by a group of Jews, the Maccabees, who were prohibited from practicing their religion by the reigning Greek government. Afterward the Temple in Jerusalem was reclaimed. Hanukkah is considered a minor holiday by rabbis because it is not mentioned in scripture, unlike Yom Kippur or Passover. Religiously speaking, the only rituals associated with it is the lighting of the *hanukiah*, a special menorah with nine candles, and the recitation of blessings.

When the triumphant Maccabees reentered the Jerusalem Temple, there was enough oil for the menorah to burn for a single day, yet the flame lasted for eight nights, or so the legend goes. That's it. A slight miracle that kick-started the "festival of lights" sometime in the second century BCE, a full two hundred years before a Jewish boy named Yeshua (Jesus) was born.

It's traditional to give small gifts to loved ones during Hanukkah, but in the last fifty years the value of those gifts has expanded exponentially for most Jewish children. Because of its proximity to Christmas, the holiday has morphed and sprawled far beyond its humble beginnings.

A few months before my conversion, Rabbi Schwartz didn't shy away from the potential quagmire Christmas represented for me. We were sitting in her office two weeks before the end of the fall semester. Having been scheduled for the mikveh that coming January, I knew where she was headed as soon as she brought the subject up.

"Are you going to see your parents for winter break?"

"Yes. You're wondering about Christmas."

"Well." She leaned back in her chair. "What are your plans?"

When I failed to produce much of an answer, she continued. "I want you to understand that for many Jews, this time of year plays out like an annual litmus test."

Memories of middle-school science experiments came back to me, those thin strips of paper that turned blue or pink, depending on what they were dipped into.

"For the majority of us," the rabbi went on, "Christmas is a reminder not of what brings us together, but of what makes us different."

"You think it's best that I no longer celebrate."

Rabbi Schwartz locked her hands behind her head. "I think you should consider it."

I studied her. How could she know what she was asking? She had never known about cheese grits and bacon, about wrapping your sister's presents. She had never known a Christmas in Houston with a brand-new pair of rollerblades, with pink laces and lightning bolts up the sides.

"Think about it, Ruth. We belong to the most liberal branch of Judaism. We have far fewer outward observances than those in the Orthodox tradition, or even the Conservatives. So for many Jews, Christmas is one of the only times each year when our separation from the greater environment comes back into focus."

"And this is a good thing?"

"Well . . ." The rabbi trailed off. "Here in America Christmas keeps arriving earlier and earlier, so for us that makes for a very long reminder. For almost two months each year we face full-on the fact that we are a minority. That, in a big way, we are not like our neighbors."

She paused to allow me to answer, but I didn't. It wasn't as if I hadn't realized I would need to give up Christmas in order to become Jewish, but my acknowledgment of this fact had remained oblique at best.

It had been far easier not to look squarely at the biggest single cultural tradition I would lose after conversion. Worse, I had assumed I had a few Christmas seasons left. Now I tried to picture the month of December without Christmas: no hymns, no faux velvet stockings, no handmade ornaments, no lights. No Advent calendars, no hidden chocolates, no Big Fake Christmas Tree.

"For those converting, it's often the hardest thing to give up."

At some point I had begun biting the inside of my cheek. I lifted my eyes to the tall shelf of books behind her desk and then met the rabbi's gaze again. God, this was deflating.

"I can give it up," I said finally.

Rabbi Schwartz's brow rose in soft relief. "Ruth. The thing that people forget is that knowing you're not like your neighbors—or in your case even like your own family—is not inherently bad. Even if it means giving up certain traditions."

She extended her hand. It didn't touch mine, but it came close. "To be reminded that you are Jewish, even if at times it is painful, can be a good thing. It can be a blessing," she paused. "If you let it."

☾

RESIGNED TO THE necessity of passing the final litmus test of Jewish conversion, I drove the eight hours north from Purdue to my parents' house in Alpena only to discover they had already decorated. So much for my fear as a girl, now my hope, that those decorations would stay hidden without my annual post-Thanksgiving fanfare.

After my father's recent promotions my mother had retired from her work in the medical field, and perhaps her new free time explained why I arrived to a house fully embellished in Christmas trimmings: glittering globes of silver throughout the kitchen, mistletoe hanging in the front foyer. The Big Fake Christmas Tree had failed to make the move from Houston to Alpena, but our chipped glass nativity scene rested on the coffee table surrounded by tea lights.

I knew my parents had not gotten a tree yet because they thought that I would want to go pick one out with Joe again, as I had since they moved to Michigan. Five years before, Joe and I had stolen our first one together (more or less). We had driven through town and hiked the jetty out over Lake Huron where a sharp wind sent the waves slamming against the stones below. That's when it came up that I had never had a real Christmas tree, a fact that astonished Joe. "Oh, you have to!" he kept saying. "You'll never go back again. Real trees smell incredible."

There was no shortage of Scots pine and Douglas fir tree farms surrounding Alpena. We left the lake and drove to a farm down the road from where Joe grew up. By then it was late, after midnight. It had stopped snowing. "I know these people," he said. "I'll leave them a check in the morning."

Off we went into the woods with a saw.

On the first Christmas I didn't celebrate, all the memories of Christmases past became too sweet to bear. That year, driving home from Joe's house one night, I forced myself to look away from the twinkling lampposts of Alpena's main street, away from the lights adorning the corner eatery, the shoe shop, the book store advertising last-minute sales. Instead I fixed my eyes straight ahead, where in the middle of the intersection a single plastic cup whipped around in the biting wind.

That year I learned how quickly, without Christmas, even a white winter loses its sheen. At the grocery store I made my visits as brief as possible, avoiding the aisles spilling over with red and green. When the local pop station began interspersing Top 40 hits with "Grandma Got Run over by a Reindeer," I turned the radio down and then off.

At the post office I was mailing a birthday card to a friend when the postmaster wished me "Merry Christmas." I cocked my head, unsure of how to respond, then walked away. Later that night I emailed a letter to the *Alpena News* about how neutral greetings would be less offensive. Not a day went by before a response to my letter was published in the same paper, from a local who told me, in so many words, to shove it.

Two days before Christmas my mom came downstairs and found me glazed over and flipping through the TV channels. Neither she nor my father had mentioned my letter to the editor or the response to it, but at around the same time some of the presents being stored near the fireplace had disappeared, only to arrive again rewrapped in blue paper. This was my mother's attempt at Hanukkah presents.

She sat down beside me. "Do you want us to get a tree?"

"I don't care."

"I could decorate it for you."

I shrugged. "Whatever. It's not my holiday anymore."

She took the remote and turned off the TV. "C'mon. Get up. I'll buy you lunch."

That year my parents didn't purchase a tree, and Joe didn't suggest cutting down one of our own. The better version of me should have been grateful for these gestures, but that December I was too busy dragging myself around Alpena like a wounded animal. The rabbi had been wrong, I thought. This was not a blessing. This was the worst part of becoming Jewish. Whenever I walked through our living room, past the corner with its absent tree, something in me cinched tight, closing around that empty space like a fist.

☾

By our first December in Replica Dodge, it had been four years since I stopped participating in Christmas. I was sitting on a couch at the Habitat for Humanity store in Ludington on a bright Saturday morning, running my hands over its red-and-gold-striped cover, when an employee approached me. She was in her sixties and wore a black turtleneck tucked into her jeans. "Are you ready for Christmas?"

"Well. That's the question."

She returned to the register, retrieving a rag to wipe down a row of brass lamps near the window. "It's surely a process," she called over her shoulder. "But you know what? That couch already looks like it's gift wrapped."

My hands came to a rest on the cover. I sat a moment longer in the couch's plush softness. Then I stood to gather my things.

"Are you interested?"

"No, thanks."

The bells on the door jingled at my exit.

If three Decembers of not celebrating Christmas hadn't made these moments easier, they had at least become more numerous, prompting my acclimation to them. If these moments still stung, the life span of each sting got shorter each year. Less and less did I carry them with me throughout the day. Less and less would they reappear hours later, pocked with the ache of absence.

Though I wasn't to the point of remembering those Houston Christmases without deep longing, I was getting skilled at knowing how to stop thinking about them. How to cut out for a long run in the hills, headphones in, how to let the dog off leash and delight in him rolling in the fresh snow. If a stranger's well-meaning greeting implied that Christmas was a holiday everyone observed—or should observe—still bothered me, it was cushioned by an increasing understanding of how towns like Alpena and Ludington operated. At least on paper, they came across as remarkably white, Christian, and conservative. Of course people assumed I celebrated Christmas. Didn't everyone around here?

"On paper"—because I, too, existed in Mason County.

Recently I'd learned about a small collective of Buddhists who met weekly for meditation in an unmarked house on Ludington's main drag. And there was a Jehovah's Witness who worked at the college's gym who didn't celebrate any holidays, and the part-time instructor with a master's in economics who was proud to say he was from Bangladesh. There were not other Jews here, but there were scores of people who for whatever reason didn't fit Mason County "on paper," and it made me wonder, that December, how many ways there were to experience otherness.

To claim that diversity didn't exist in Mason County was a lie, even if at times the opposite seemed true. It was a lie that erased my own experiences. Perhaps this is what the rabbi had been talking about. *To be reminded that, in a big way, we are not like our neighbors.* Was there anyone in Mason County who did not know what it was like to feel out of place? Even for just a moment? Even just a little?

The more I thought about that question, the more convinced I became that even if the Mason County stereotype did exist—someone who was perfectly white, perfectly conservative, and perfectly Christian—that person was, as Socrates would have it, experiencing "an unexamined life." Everyone around me, even those who seemed to fit in flawlessly, had at some point felt like a stranger. In their own town, in their own homes. The alienation I experienced around Christmas each year was not a Jewish condition. It was a human one.

Each person in Mason County had experienced, was experiencing, or would experience isolation at some point, in known and unknown ways. It was impossible to count, ubiquitous and singular and infinite. Or as the Jewish Kabbalists would call it, *Ein Sof.* "Without End."

Another name for God.

☾

THERE WAS A knock at the door of my office and I opened up to find Jen. I pointed out the window. "Can you believe this?"

Outside the latest winter squall had picked up speed and was barreling down snow in sheets that made it hard to see fifty feet beyond the glass. I wasn't looking forward to the drive home. Then I noticed a large wicker basket in Jen's hands. "What's that?"

"These are yours."

"Mine?"

"For Hanukkah. A gift for each night. The first night is tonight, right?"

I looked at the basket and back at Jen. Eight gifts. Each with an earth-inspired decoration, a slip of birch bark, a red wax seal, baker's twine used as ribbon. Jen lifted one item from basket and placed it in my hands.

I pulled at the ribbon until a block of fine soap came tumbling out. I lifted it to my nose and inhaled. Sandalwood. "Where did you get this?"

"The organic shop downtown. Don't get too excited," Jen said as she moved past me to set the basket on my desk. "All your gifts are small. From the reading I've done, that's true to Hanukkah's roots."

My first impulse was to throw my arms around her, but having been close with Jen for almost a year now, I was well acquainted with the perpetual sphere of personal space that seemed to encapsulate my best friend. She had a steadfast reserve that caused even those who knew her well to think twice before going in for a hug. The single time I had tried embracing Jen before, she had gone stiff, giving me instead three firm pats on the back.

"I know gift giving isn't one of Joe's strong suits," she said. "I just thought someone should honor you in this way."

I smelled the sandalwood soap again.

I wondered if she could tell I was on the verge of tears.

"You want a hug, don't you?" Jen wrinkled her nose. Then she opened her arms.

That evening it had stopped snowing by the time I climbed into Joe's truck to head home. I placed Jen's basket of gifts on the seat next to me and thought about the time it must have taken her to choose the gifts, and the research she had done, and the careful wrapping of each gift. Had I never moved to Mason County, there would be no Jen in my life. Had my parents never left Houston, there would be no Joe. Both natives of Michigan, both raised on the rural outskirts of those twinning towns of Ludington and Alpena, in a way they were like brother and sister. There was something constant between them, something shared.

Listening was one of the purest ways to shift back into the present, I was learning that December, my fourth without Christmas. This time of year the land became so hushed that one had to actively listen to avoid buying into some stereotypical rural winter silence, so I would come home and listen to the land. I would get out of the grocery store, that palace of red and green, and let the road carry the truck over asphalt, then gravel, then dirt. Greet the dog and let him out, watch him run into the bare cherry orchard. Rifle season was winding down and gunshots were rare. One day I came home to find the wind had blown down a whole section of fence in Replica Dodge, but I decided it looked better that way, and vowed to dig up the rest come spring.

There was some consolation in that thought, too, the idea of breaking earth.

People around here often said there was something ineffable about living in the deep countryside. The tourist driving down these dirt roads probably felt lonely looking at these old farmhouses, perhaps even pity for the people inside, but to those who lived there, it was the opposite. The woods and fields were an emptiness that filled you up. They were nourishing and welcoming.

That night when I got home I located the small blue box of Hanukkah candles I'd bought from the German Baptist mercantile. (They had called us with their answer by then—yes to borrowing the banquet tables—but could a few of them attend, please? They had never been to a Jewish wedding. We invited them instantly.) From the hutch in our living room, I retrieved my menorah and set it on the table closest to the window overlooking Replica Dodge.

Baruch atah, Adonai Eloheinu, Melech haolam, asher kid'shanu, b'mizvotav, v'tsivanu l'hadlik ner shel Hanukkah, I began.

Blessed are you, Adonai our God, who hallows us with *mitzvot*, commanding us to kindle the Hannukah lights. I continued in Hebrew. Blessed are you, Adonai our God, Sovereign of all, who performed wondrous deeds for our ancestors in days of old at this season. Blessed are you, Adonai our God, Sovereign of all, for giving us life, for sustaining us, and for enabling us to reach this season.

With the final blessing I lit the helper candle and lifted it to light the candle for the first night. Looking back outside, for the first time it struck me that there were no Christmas trees I could see shining in other people's windows. There were no Christmas lights within range. Here in Replica Dodge there was only night sky, fresh snow, and the dark-on-dark where the barn rose against the hardwoods. In front of me, inside me, two flames flickered.

11

THE COLD MONTHS

WINTER DRIVING MEANT mastering the art of vehicular minimalism. In the truck I reminded myself to accelerate gradually, to take turns by the inch. *Can't remember the last time I went over forty-five,* mumbled a student coming into class late, having braved the latest winter storm. She was right. At least on the back roads of Mason County, some of which seemed to be plowed only at random, accelerating beyond forty-five was like asking for an accident. For most of my students, by now, the snow had lost its sexiness. The holidays were over. Now there was nothing to do but wait for the end of March.

Yet even in deep winter there were a few mornings of full sun when the temperature threatened to scramble back up and hold, and it gave us, if not hope, at least some twinges of optimism. On these days my students could peek out of the class windows and watch the snow melt off their car hoods. They seemed more alive, engaged, openly dreaming about miles of black asphalt under their tires for the ride home. So much of winter in Mason County seemed to come down to that: speaking about wishes and fears.

And driving carefully. *Don't jump the gas*, I told myself. *Don't jump the brake.*

The sun was hardly visible most of the time, and ice coated the rural hills around Replica Dodge. For me that ice held the status of a keepsake, created and re-created, a souvenir of a trip Joe and I had taken to Alpena two years prior. Post-college poor, we had just landed in Mason County, and with both of us working only part-time at the college, there had been no money for snow tires.

True to form, in making the trip, Joe had opted for the wooded highway over the freeways. We were driving our old Benz, which was rusting from beneath. It was not late but dark already, as happens in January in Michigan, when the sun sets half an hour after 5.

We were headed east on a two-way road when I heard a stark *whoosh*, as if for a split second our car had been lifted clean off the pavement. Then we were spiraling across the midline into the other lane. I grabbed the door handle and braced for impact while Joe kept saying over and over, as the car spun, *We're okay, we're okay, we're okay*, as if saying so were enough to secure some ideal outcome.

We were okay. By the time the Benz stopped spinning we had completed a three-sixty and faced oncoming traffic on the sharp curve, but it was the backcountry and there was no traffic. The car's tires had dug into the slush on one side of the road and its headlights illuminated the white mess of earth the Benz had spit up in its twisting. I was cold but grateful, especially when a pair of hunters came by a half hour later and hauled us out with all the essentials we didn't have: a tow line and four-wheel drive. They opened their thermoses and poured hot coffee into our travel mugs, shook our hands, and we were back on the road.

Now I knew there was nothing special about that night. Everyone in Mason County has a story like ours, or worse. Black ice, sharp curve, *couldn't-see-two-feet-in-front-of-me* wintry mix. In taking the icy hills slowly, I began to think about rites of passage again. In Michigan, spinning off the road in winter just meant that I had been here long enough to begin to belong.

☾

IF WE WANTED to host the reception in the barn by June, renovations had to start in March. The indoor deer blind needed to come out. The bar needed to be built. There were beams that could use extra support and floorboards that needed lapping over, all of which meant that the initial cleaning out of the barn—of its heaps of trinkets and trash, rickety lawn ornaments and Replica Dodge leftovers—was a task we could no longer avoid.

It was the middle of February and we had the week off. We watched as the local waste company eased an enormous dumpster onto the driveway leading up to our barn. The night before the wind had sent the snow sidelong across the yard, leaving Replica Dodge's church steeple packed on one side but naked on the other. It was the kind of trickster snow that for the briefest moment held you on the surface before swallowing you up to the knees. My students were right. The snow's appeal was waning.

The Skiptons probably thought we were crazy. They drove by and slowed down, puzzled to see us working outside at the worst time of the year. Joe and I kept hoping the sun would emerge, but that week the clouds stayed low and thick, and soon the dumpster contained almost as much snow as trash, meaning each morning we began by climbing into it to shovel out the previous night's snow.

On the fourth day I started to think, *We are crazy.*

The sheer expanse of dust, rodent spines, and shit we discovered in the process of working through the barn's colossal piles was staggering. Under twelve boxes of broken mason jars, lying on top of Bill's old workshop, we found an entire rusting automatic garage door. The broad orange net that was spread out over it had served as the communal bathroom for the barn's wild animal population, and given the amount of shit, I was shocked we didn't see them scurrying off in every imaginable direction.

In another corner of the barn we discovered a frame for an above-ground pool, surrounded by bags of chlorine and strips of stained carpet. Had Bill been planning to add a pool to Replica Dodge? In the lofts and on the floor, shoved onto shelves and leaning against corners and walls, more junk, trinkets, and animal remnants. Under Bill's indoor deer blind I lifted a box of *TV Guides* to find a possum carcass blackened with decay.

We heaved and hauled and shook out and sledge-hammered and swept and shoveled our way through the barn. The temperature hovered in the high teens that week, but for whatever reason, despite knowing the work ahead, neither of us had prepared by purchasing proper gloves. I'd bought some mittens earlier in the season, and we had other gloves for summer yard chores, but we now discovered the need for a third type, working winter gloves. The type of gloves worn by people who own barns.

But Joe and I became so busy with the task at hand that we never got around to purchasing those gloves. That week we hardly went into town, and instead improvised. From a cabinet full of trowels and Miracle-Gro, Joe unearthed a bright yellow pair of gardening gloves and christened them "the Olajuwons," a tribute to Hakeem, one of my favorite players for the Houston Rockets. They were three times too big for his hands. My own winter mittens weren't much thicker. Every morning there was the tender period between when my fingers became cold and when they went numb. They were more useful after going numb, I learned. More ignorable.

Finally the barn was cleared. We had filled the dumpster to its brim. Joe was still sporting the Olajuwons when, at the end of the day, at the end of that week, I found him wrestling two of Bill's pink poolside lounging chairs back out of the dumpster.

"What are you doing?"

He set the two of them up on the barn's porch. It was freezing outside, but for the moment the snow had stopped. I was exhausted. Six days of cleaning the barn had made stacking a season's worth of wood seem like child's play. I was ready for a hot shower and a few hours of guilty-pleasure TV.

"Sit with me," he said.

I studied the broken chairs. They had kinked aluminum frames and their seats were made of bright plastic ribbon in a cross-stitch pattern. It was one I remembered well: on a hot day in Houston, a chair like that stuck to your thighs and left its mark. Bill's chairs were frayed at the edges, and for the hundredth time that week, a fear of exposure to potential pathogens struck me. Tetanus, E. coli. We had worn masks, we had been diligent about washing our hands, but would that be enough?

"Okay."

I waited as Joe disappeared into the house and reemerged with two shots of whiskey. He leaned into the wind, trudging through the snow to get back to the barn porch, and we sank into the poolside chairs.

"It's possible I'm covered everywhere," I announced, "in a thin stratum of possum shit."

Joe laughed as he adjusted his chair to the furthest reclined position. Hearing him laugh made me realize I hadn't heard that sound for almost a week. I had missed it. We stared up at the metal ceiling of the barn porch.

"This is crazy. Who cleans their barn in the middle of February?"

Joe sipped his whiskey. Then he leaned over and kissed my neck.

I raised my glass, and just then the snow began to fall again. Our backs to the emptied barn, our bodies gone soft from the work, we said little more. We stayed in the lounge chairs for a long time.

☾

I KEPT THINKING about Rabbi Menshov's refusal to marry us, and this made me recall all the rabbis in my past, beginning with the warmth of Jeff Kleinman, whose class at the University of Houston had introduced me to Judaism. Then Rabbi Illana Schwartz, my conversion sponsor, who could never be called warm, but whose formality had challenged me to examine how I would sustain my Jewish identity going forward. Did I know the seriousness of the commitment I was about to make? Was I prepared to forego other traditions? Would I establish a Jewish home?

Rabbi Schwartz had made it clear that when I emerged from the freezing transformation of the mikveh, I emerged a Jew. I thought about the other rabbis I had been contacting, drafting email upon email: *Though we've never met, I'm hoping that once you hear about my situation, you'll be open to the possibility of officiating at an interfaith wedding.* I had received no responses. Then there was Rabbi Menshov of Grand Rapids, who did return my call, only to promptly refuse to oversee a wedding between a Jew and a non-Jew.

As the head of a Conservative congregation, Menshov's refusal was not only typical but required. This simple fact I would learn only later, after digging further into the issue of interfaith marriage at InterfaithFamily, a resource organization started in Chicago. Of the four major movements in modern American Judaism, only two allowed rabbis to officiate at interfaith marriages: Reform (my own branch) and Reconstructionist Judaism. Yet in Reform, I learned, the largest of the denominations, rabbis were still discouraged from officiating at interfaith weddings, meaning that even the ones who could perform interfaith weddings were likely to reject such requests.

Perhaps this was why I hadn't picked up the phone to call Rabbi Schwartz. Something told me she would say no. A similar hesitation had kept me from asking any of the other rabbis I knew and respected—but this, too, was normal. Among my Jewish friends at the University of Houston, one told me that if she married outside the religion, she wouldn't even bother asking the rabbi at her lifelong synagogue. She expected to be refused.

This was not an ignorant convert's problem. This was a religion-wide issue.

Then one morning, finally, a reply.

> *Dear Natalie,*
> *Thank you for contacting me about your wedding, and mazel tov on your engagement. I very much support interfaith*

couples and would be pleased to do everything I can to make your wedding a meaningful experience, both for the two of you and your families.

I read and reread the message, then ran to get Joe. Here was Rabbi David Zamenhof.

☾

FOR YEARS AFTERWARD I would remember Rabbi Zamenhof as a maverick. As someone who, in my brief history with Judaism, at once conformed to and strayed far from what I had come to expect of rabbis. A native Chicagoan, he was in his fifties, but had a boyish face. He was the head of a congregation in Lansing, Michigan.

For our first meeting via Skype I dressed as if attending temple services—Joe in a button-up beside me—but the rabbi clicked into view sporting a white T-shirt. This threw me, yet as he took notes during that meeting, I noticed a richly embroidered *yarmulke* resting on the crown of his head. He told us he was a graduate of the Reconstructionist Rabbinical College in Philadelphia.

Reconstructionist is the fourth branch of Judaism beyond America's more prominent movements: Reform, Conservative, and Orthodox. Kleinman had mentioned the Reconstructionists during his introductory class in his genial and offhand way— *No one's sure what they believe, but they're part of us*—but Rabbi Zamenhof had no problem putting this belief into words. At the core of Reconstructionism, he explained, was the acknowledgment of each generation's right to reshape the religion, because only through purposeful revision could Judaism remain meaningful in modern life.

As far as I could tell, it was the branch of choice for Jews who had a hard time with old rules. I told him about my past.

"We could do a better job of encouraging those in the conversion process," Rabbi Zamenhof told me.

"I'm not so sure. Isn't it beneficial to have a long period of study?"

"Study, yes, but we miss the point when Judaism becomes more exclusive than inclusive. Like this situation. When rabbis refuse to officiate at a marriage between a Jew and non-Jew, they risk isolating both parties."

He put down his pen and started gesticulating wildly. "How can we be surprised when, in the coming years, the couple does not bring their children back to temple? If we reject them at the marriage altar, we have lost them. That includes their future children."

Much of what Rabbi Zamenhof said during that first meeting was supported by the linked articles, messages, and news briefs on his congregation's website. Zamenhof had led an interfaith Thanksgiving service in Lansing, and he had addressed the Unity with Diversity program at the Islamic Center. He had published an article through InterfaithFamily called "Providing Comfort to ALL Who Mourn."

Clearly inclusion was a flashpoint for Zamenhof in a big-tent Judaism way, but this impulse extended beyond religion. The *Lansing State Journal* later reported on a vigil held against Muslim hate speech where Zamenhof spoke alongside a local imam. A feature image captured the rabbi in plain clothes, surrounded by a crowd, a megaphone against his mouth.

☾

As EXCITED AS I was about Zamenhof officiating our ceremony, communicating with him reminded me of a moment toward the end of my mikveh ceremony I hated to remember.

After most of those in attendance had filed out of the room, Rabbi Schwartz and I sat on a couch together sifting through documents.

"Here is the original," she said, giving me the contract I had signed moments earlier. "I'll send this copy to the American Jewish Archives in Cincinnati."

"Thanks." I took it from her.

"Consider yourself registered. On the books as Jewish." Then Rabbi Schwartz smiled.

I was surprised. I returned her smile but as soon as I did, hers was gone.

Rabbi Schwartz brought the copies to rest in her lap. "Ruth, there is something you should understand. Should you choose to disclose it, the vast majority of Jews will accept the major process we've just completed."

"Yes?"

"To me you are a Jew. But unfortunately I'm obligated to tell you that for some—few and far between—this process will not be enough."

She lifted her face again. Something amounting to pity was washing over it.

I was confused. "What do you mean?"

The question hung in the air, and she did not attempt to answer me.

"You mean that to some Jews I'm still not Jewish?"

Even as I spoke the words, I couldn't make sense of them. As if I hadn't just spent years attending services, reading Jewish history, studying maps, learning Hebrew prayers, observing new holidays and canceling Christmas forever from my future.

"After everything?"

"Fools," Rabbi Schwartz mumbled.

She slipped my conversion documents into an envelope and sealed it. Then she changed the topic so quickly that her revelation—one she had clearly saved until after my conversion was complete—skipped like a stone across the surface of that day, that day like the water of the mikveh itself, still and bright and reflective, essential to my life.

Only now, in Replica Dodge, did that stone cut through and sink deep. Still not Jewish.

Here was the truth: I knew the people she was talking about. I had met them before. Their way of thinking went like this: my father and mother were not Jewish. No amount of study could remedy this. No amount of participation. No honest commitment. No immersion. To these Jews I would never be Jewish enough. I would remain an oddity, just as to some Christians my conversion had rendered me devious. Lost. A person to avoid.

Faced with this memory, I returned to Zamenhof's welcome message on his congregation's website. I wanted it, too, to sink in like a stone.

I hope never to forget that each person sees a different face of God. The Torah I revere is the Torah that unites humanity and tramples cruelty. This is the Torah that, according to Rabbi Yishma'el, is given to us in order to "smash the ear." While the ear attuned to the literal and mundane hears separateness in the words of the Torah, the ear that has been "smashed open" by the text itself hears the still, small voice of love, wisdom, and possibility.

☾

BY THE MIDDLE of March the barn was a different building. Empty and open, it reminded me even more of the Rothko Chapel. With each passing day the sunlight lasted longer, until all of Replica Dodge dripped, its wood darkened by melted snow rushing off the roofs and collecting as tiny puddles in the windowsills of the church, saloon, and general store. Tiny puddles that overflowed to make a beeline for the grass.

Grass. I could see it now. More and more of it.

My students had warned me. *Don't expect too much. Warm one day, snow the next.*

Warm in West Michigan, I gleaned, was any day in March when the temperature stayed above forty degrees.

I tried not to get excited, telling myself that the snow would return, but then it stayed above forty degrees for six days straight. Under the warming sun, Joe's truck became a miniature greenhouse in the college's parking lot, toasty to climb into after a day of teaching. Deer congregated to lick salt off the sides of the back roads. With almost a week of milder temps, it seemed as if winter had gone down for good. I began wearing skirts without leggings and painting my toenails again, and in the mornings the dog and I dashed our three miles across the reexposed earth, mud splattering our hindquarters.

After these runs I would remove my shoes on the porch and smack them together just to watch the dirt spit off into the yard. It was a welcome sight and gradually, despite my suspicions, I started to trust that March warmth. For the first time in my life I had the strong urge to plant something, anything I could sink my teeth into by the end of July.

Of course the following week reminded me that my students were right. The ground was still too hard to plant anything. Then the temperature plummeted.

We were reading Orwell's "Shooting an Elephant" and one of my students remarked that the elephant's protracted death reminded her of winter in West Michigan. "It never collapses in one clean and dignified moment," she said. "It's just like Orwell wrote it. Here winter sags to its knees and stands up again. It slobbers at the mouth. Face it, Ms. Joynton, our elephant takes a long time to die."

On the week of Passover, everything went white again.

Passover, the major eight-day festival that celebrates Jewish freedom from slavery, is like no other Jewish holiday. This is because Passover is a time warp. No other celebration in the Jewish calendar compares to Passover, because of this idea that what happened then is happening now, is always happening to Jews everywhere. A fight for freedom, a going out and forth. There is specific emphasis during Passover to imagine oneself not as separate from those ancient Jews, but as one of them. Free. Rushing into the desert. Hopeful, terrified. Hot.

Yet I shivered anytime the door was opened, and this fact reminded me of the other characteristic of the annual holiday: Passover's contradictory nature. Passover is a time when practicing Jews give up leavened bread for a week to eat *matzah*—slave bread, because you are what you eat—and yet the annual Seder, often enjoyed with one's congregation or family, doesn't seem impoverished, but carries with it a sense of opulence and warmth.

Someone once explained the Passover Seder to me as the Jewish Thanksgiving, and between the singing, the four cups of wine, and the lengthy retelling of the Exodus story, I can see why. Passover is about blurring lines and pronouns, when *they* become *us, we* become *them*. The holiday accentuates time's circular, rather than linear, features.

Above all Passover is about the survival of Jews, and so it's also a love song. This is why it's not uncommon to hear readings from the Song of Solomon.

> *Come, my beloved, let us go out into the fields,*
> *to lie among the henna-bushes;*
> *let us go early to the vineyards*
> *and see if the vine has budded*
> *or its blossom opened,*
> *if the pomegranates are in flower.*

Yeah, right, I thought, looking out at Replica Dodge.

☾

THE LATE SNOW didn't seem to faze Joe or Rich, his father, who was visiting that week to continue our work on the barn. Together they ripped the remaining paneling off the walls, revealing more of the original boards.

With the roads covered again in ice and snow, my morning run with the dog had broken back down into a slow amble. I kept telling myself that a gradual spring was good for the cherry farmers, or so I had heard. It was good for the Mannens who owned the orchard across from Replica Dodge. Just last year they had lost their entire crop when the spring had become too warm, too soon, and for too long. The blossoms had burst forth only to perish in the following frost.

For Passover it's tradition to clean one's house. To rid it of *chametz,* or leavened bread. As the well-known story goes, after

Pharaoh freed the Jews, Moses led them out of Egypt so quickly their bread had no time to rise. Instead they baked it into a hard flat sustenance called matzah, a simple mixture of flour and water that tastes dry and sweet.

I had planned on performing this ritual, but as Passover drew closer, I kept bumping up against considerable uncertainty. At first I thought it was related to the barn, the fact that I had just spent a week finishing the most disgusting cleaning task ever. Another extensive clean sounded awful, and this was the reason for my dawdling. Then a few more days passed and I began to chalk up my procrastination to something else.

There was a more obvious reason why I was keeping our cereals, muffins, and crackers in the pantry. After his thirty-plus years in building maintenance, Joe's father had retired with a body that recalled every major installation, repair, and renovation project he had ever completed. I could see it in the way he moved about our farmhouse, the sharp breaths he sometimes sucked in as he straightened up from retrieving a fork knocked off the table. Rich's hands were huge, roughened by work, and some of his fingernails were permanently damaged. His knees gave him trouble.

Like Joe, he was a beautiful man, well built and quiet, smart, raised Catholic. He wasn't always in pain and when he was, he did his best to hide it, but I knew that the work he had come to do—the repairs to our barn—took a toll on him. Yet here he was with his tools, his decades of expertise. Somehow, as Passover closed in and as I watched him head out to the barn with his son each morning, the idea of cleaning all the bread out of our house grew more and more intimidating.

I didn't bring this up with Joe. If I was having trouble ridding my house of chametz and getting into the Passover spirit, it was my own problem, not one for my atheist fiancé to wade through with me. Joe had promised to support me in my Jewish faith, but somehow that didn't seem to extend to areas of the faith where I still had fears and uncertainty.

Years later I would discover a bevy of Passover recipes, from apple kugel to chocolate-dipped matzah, from masala roasted chicken to rich spinach quiche, designed for those keeping kosher. Free of chametz, these were recipes passed down by Jewish families for generations: Moroccan Shabbat fish, beef brisket, Passover pizza, noodleless lasagna that promised to taste even better than the standard version. One search on Google would've turned up thousands of meals and the possibility that I—and maybe even Joe's father—would hardly have noticed the absence of bread at our farmhouse table.

Over hundreds of years, through constant culinary invention, the Jews had transformed the festival's most notable constraint into a multitude of feasts. If this wasn't survivorship, what was? But that first March in Replica Dodge, I didn't even know to look for those recipes because I had never seen them prepared. I had tasted them at Passover Seders at various synagogues, but I had never been behind the scenes, in the kitchen. Now the real reason for my hesitation reared up. I didn't know how to rid my house of chametz because I had never witnessed the ritual carried out firsthand.

This cleaning ritual, done inside the home and distinct from the temple, presented some other piece of Judaism that remained foreign to me. Like vines traveling the length of a great trunk, this practice circled the religion but remained outside of temple life. This practice had to do with family. I didn't know the steps of cleaning for Passover—or even how to begin to feel familiar with them—because this practice had played no part in my own family's history.

Rabbi Schwartz had called them fools, but maybe they weren't. Maybe those Jews for whom I would never be Jewish enough were on to something, because no amount of Hebrew prayers or Shabbat services or observance of holidays could give me the one thing I would never have: a Jewish childhood.

Once almost out of the blue Rabbi Kleinman had told me, "The crazy thing is, Ruth, if you complete your conversion, you'll probably know more about Judaism than many practicing today." Kleinman had said this with a degree of sadness, but at the time his statement had sparked the opposite in me, a vague hope that I could eventually fit in seamlessly. But he had been talking about the religion of Judaism. When it came to Jewish culture, a history that I could never claim, how could I hope to be anything but an eternal student?

In Mason County it was impossible to hide my lack of Jewish culture within the kindness of a congregation. A congregation like the one I'd known as a graduate student at Temple Emanu-El, whose families would invite me into their homes for resplendent Passover Seders. This time of year did not take me back to a tradition of matzah and Moroccan Shabbat fish. It took me back to Mardi Gras season in Texas. It took me back to plastic baby Jesuses hidden inside king cakes, to egg hunts on the church lawn, to the bright beads thrown at women who flashed their boobs at the Galveston parade.

☾

TOWARD THE END of the month, Rabbi Zamenhof met us again over Skype. He had asked us to find meaningful quotes for our wedding ceremony, and Joe offered his first, a quote from Albert Einstein. "Gravitation cannot be held responsible for people falling in love. How on earth can you explain, in terms of chemistry and physics, so important a biological phenomenon as love? Put your hand on a stove for a minute and it seems like an hour. Sit with that special girl for an hour and it seems like a minute. That's relativity."

Zamenhof nodded. "Good."

Then I read mine. It was a quote from Rilke. "A merging of two people is an impossibility, and where it seems to exist, it is a hemming in," I began.

The passage was from a letter Rilke had written to a young man about the point of marriage *not* being the melding of separate individuals, and I continued. "Even between the two closest people infinite distances exist, but a marvelous living side-by-side can grow up for them, if they succeed in loving the expanse between them."

I looked back at Joe, who seemed skeptical. Rabbi Zamenhof became pensive. "Loving the expanse between them," he repeated. "Loving the expanse. You know, usually couples are trying convince everyone that they're perfect for one another on the wedding day."

"Not perfect," I said.

Joe softened. "Just done hiding."

The rabbi beamed.

12

IN HOLINESS

THE DUST OF the cedar mulch I was spreading tickled my nostrils and made me cough. It was less than a month before the wedding and our days were spent working outside. Joe was putting the finishing touches on the barn while I swept Bill's buildings, planted flowers, and mulched beds. Later that day, at the seamstress's house, I stared at myself in the full-length mirror, my simple dress pinned for one last cut.

This is it, I thought.

In the frantic fifty-degree weeks before the wedding, I was beginning to understand what James Skipton had meant by "that much work." We were trying to make Replica Dodge look like the Skiptons'—clean, warm, perfectly trimmed, lined with blooms, something approximating an actual wedding venue—but this was beyond impractical. It was downright stupid. It was impossible on multiple fronts: for one, we could do nothing to normalize

Replica Dodge, Bill's proud western town standing among the cherry orchards.

Still I toiled, trying to re-create the better stereotypes of rural living for our guests, all bucolic views and field mice, nary a wildflower out of place. I wanted to give them the best version of Michigan I could muster, and the more I worked, the more the effort struck me as both defensive and protective and exactly, I realized one night, what a local would do.

I had done this before, but for Houston. For years I had assured outsiders that the city was far more diverse than people's dated idea of it. The work for Replica Dodge stemmed from the same place. By the end of the month, thanks to Rich and Joe, the barn looked like a place the tourists would rent for their own ceremonies, walls and sides returned to the original beams, floor repaired, a bar finished from Bill's old workshop bench. Joe hung a pair of handmade chandeliers from the ceiling. When switched on, they bathed the space below in gold.

The college semester was ending but by now I knew that when it came to Mason County, the semester ending didn't mean the end of students. That May it seemed like I ran into them everywhere.

"Is it just me, or does it seem like we can't go anyplace without running into former students?" I asked Joe.

"I know. The numbers increase with each passing term. And we've been here some time now."

This is it, I thought again.

To celebrate turning in grades we went out to the local brewery with our colleagues. The conversation grew boisterous, the laughter loud, and by the end of the night I was fighting an uncanny urge to do something foolish. Really foolish. I wasn't sure if it was the beer, or the wedding, but I found myself fantasizing about trespassing on private property. Doing flips off some kid's trampoline, the whole lot of us. I wanted to go for a late-night swim in Lake Michigan and chance the undertow.

But I knew better. I knew how that night would end. We would each have one drink, two at the most, a good meal, and finish with some coffee before the drive home. Our colleagues were older and most were married. There were husbands, wives, and children waiting. All of them had long adapted to these tremendous responsibilities. We were next. A former student of one of us would bring the check and we would tip well, regardless of whether they had failed or passed our class.

The Chicago tourists were returning and the grocery stores were starting to stock summer ale varieties again, with their traces of oranges and lemons, but that May proved intractable in its coolness. One night, a week before the wedding, I awoke in a panic. I had been dreaming of cherries, ripe in my hands. I got out of bed and put on a sweater and went to stand outside in the dark.

I stared at the trees across the road. For several nights, the temperature had hovered back down around freezing. In the moonlight I could see that the trees were just beginning to send forth their pink buds. Already I could smell their sweetness, but in the back of my mind I couldn't help but also hear the farmers. Would this year be like last year? Would the cherries blossom, only to die in the frost?

☾

THE BREAKING OF the glass is the most well-known of any Jewish wedding tradition. Originally designed to commemorate the destruction of the Temple in Jerusalem, even as its meanings have diversified over the centuries, it has almost always served as a reminder—to the couple and to guests—that even in life's most joyful moments, sorrow remains.

Some see the breaking of the glass as a commemoration of all the sufferings Jewish people have endured throughout history, while others view it as a symbol of the nature of marriage itself: fragile and dependent on the promises made on one's wedding day, which, if shattered, renders the bond between two people virtually irreparable.

On the day before the wedding we picked up the banquet tables from the German Baptists. The process of securing them had been absurd, but as I looked at them arranged in the renovated barn, I couldn't help but feel glad we had seen that saga through.

We had made it through our first year at Replica Dodge.

It was late when the closest of our friends and family left that evening. As the last car's lights disappeared down the dirt road, I found Joe on the porch, looking out into the city.

"Are you nervous?" I asked.

"Nah."

"I am."

"I know." Joe waggled his eyebrows at me.

A few days before a small package had arrived at our house. The black velvet bag inside held the thin glass Joe would break at the end of our ceremony. But something else had come with it too, something I had not told Joe about. The Israeli vendor had also sent a hand-stitched yarmulke wound around the black velvet bag. An extra of sorts, a good-luck token. I hadn't ordered it but it was beautiful, and from the moment I held it in my hand, I had been thinking about Joe wearing it. Just for the ceremony, just once.

I had been thinking about it but had said nothing. I went back into the farmhouse and opened the living room hutch where I had tucked the yarmulke away. I thumbed the soft circle of it in my hand. I thought about the person who had sewn it, and the long trek the *kippah* had made from Israel to Mason County, Michigan. Then I headed back out to the porch. "This came a few days ago," I said, handing it to him. "With the glass."

Joe held it up in the porch light.

"You don't have to wear it if you don't want to." I paused to allow him to respond. He didn't. "But it would mean a great deal to me. Just for the ceremony."

Joe smoothed the fabric with his fingers. "Don't you have to be Jewish to wear one of these?"

"No. That's a misconception. It's a sign of respect."

I sat down beside him. "Please. For the rest of our lives, we will go back to this day. The images, the words, the people present."

"And you need this as part of that memory?"

"Maybe. I don't know. Holding the yarmulke just makes me think about the future."

"Future?"

"Children. They won't come for a few years, but they won't have the memories that we'll make tomorrow. They'll have a few images. That's it."

Joe turned back to Replica Dodge. I turned and stared out with him.

"It was one of the commitments I made, Joe. To raise them as Jews."

Joe picked up the yarmulke. "This one's nice."

"Do you know how to wear it?"

Joe shook his head. "No."

"Tomorrow there will be plenty of people here who can help you—"

Joe held up his hand. He folded the yarmulke and tucked it into the pocket of his pants. "Let me think about it, okay?"

☾

HIGH CLOUDS SPECKLED the blue above Replica Dodge, turning out just enough of a breeze to rid the Skiptons' meadow, where we would marry, of black flies. It was seventy-two degrees and the hours before the ceremony rushed by in a blur of vendors assembling tents, positioning kegs, and setting up speakers. Friends combed the property for sweet pea and honeysuckle to finish off the floral centerpieces.

A sea of familiar faces descended upon Replica Dodge. Wishes, jokes, and advice seemed to pour forth from everyone. My relatives from Texas elbowed me and joked, *Girl, you talk like you're from Michigan now.* My Southern Baptist grandfather called from his hospital bed to say, *I hope he is the ideal husband. God's blessings upon you. If only Mary Ruth were here today . . .* My mother wrapped me in her arms and whispered, *My last baby, my last baby.*

It was my father's job to periodically check on me and make sure I had enough to eat. He kept urging me to take a few moments for myself in the midst of the clamor. Those few moments finally arrived in the bathroom of the farmhouse an hour before the ceremony. It was early evening and the house was almost empty, most of the helpers having gone back into town to shower and dress before returning with the rest of the guests. I sighed and sank down into a chair near the window, peeling the clothes from my body. My simple dress hung on the back of the bathroom door, and I was suddenly grateful that I had decided against having bridesmaids. It was just me now, I thought. Thank God. And that's when I saw it.

Inside my belly button was a tick.

Chills sprang through me. Lunging toward the medicine cabinet for something, anything, to get it off, I found some tweezers, but when I sat back down and tried to lift it up, the tick's tiny legs began to wriggle.

I lobbed the tweezers across the room and yanked my robe off the hanger, still struggling into it as I charged out of the bathroom to where the caterer was setting up. "I need to speak to Joe," I said, trying to keep the panic out of my voice. "The groom. Right now. Please find him for me."

Back in the bathroom, I slid down the wall by the cabinet to the floor.

Ten minutes later there was a knock on the door.

"Are you in there? Natalie? You can open up. It's me."

I unlocked the door. Joe looked like he hadn't showered yet. He was carrying a hammer.

"Oh, my God. Why are you dirty and still hammering?"

I untied my robe.

"Ah," he smiled. "Sure."

"No!" I pointed. "Look at my belly button! There's a tick in it!"

Joe bent down. "Huh."

He squinted and studied the insect for a moment, then stood back up and retrieved the tweezers I had thrown across the room. He bent down again. I cringed.

He pulled the tick off and held it up to the light, examining it. "It's nowhere near engorged. That's good. You probably won't get Lyme disease."

"Thanks. That *is* good news. As a little girl I always dreamed of not getting Lyme disease on the day I got married."

Joe dropped the tick into the toilet and flushed, and together we watched it circle the bowl until it disappeared. I retied my robe and shuddered.

Joe put his arm around me. "You know there's a tick species named after your home state. After Texas. It's called the Lone Star tick. We don't have them here in Michigan, so actually we have fewer tick species here. Just FYI. Also I've decided to wear the yarmulke."

God. Only Joe would know about some tick species native to Texas, where he had never lived. Only Joe would attempt to educate me on Lone Star ticks minutes before we exchanged vows. Suddenly I started laughing.

"Never a dull moment." I kissed him. "Thanks. I'll see you under the chuppah."

☾

AFTER RABBI ZAMENHOF's blessings we drank from the kiddush cup, and the Rilke and Einstein quotes were read. We exchanged rings and vows—Joe saying, *You are bound to me in holiness*, and me repeating, *You are bound to me in holiness*—and then came the breaking of the glass and the great *Mazel tov!* that echoed through the hardwoods.

From the Skiptons' field everyone returned to Replica Dodge, to the barn and the tent set up outside for dinner, drinks, and dancing. Evening became late evening, and late evening became, before I knew it, deep night.

In another rare moment to myself, I watched as guests snapped photos of the tables, beams, and lights, as they scurried from building to building in Replica Dodge, their cell phone cameras flashing to illuminate Bill's saloon, schoolhouse, and the Lady's Emporium.

I studied their faces for some urban smugness, but found none. Bill's city amazed them.

"Every day I spend two hours in traffic," a guest wandered up to me to say. "What a waste when there are places like this."

"Your property reminds me of your great-grandmother's dairy farm in Louisiana," an uncle mentioned. "That big magnolia in the back with its white petals."

"Do you get any cherries when they're ripe?" friends from Houston asked. "Do you ever miss Texas? I would miss the food, but Houston construction is getting out of control."

"I don't know if I could live here," remarked a former boss. "But I never knew a lake could look like an ocean."

At the end of the evening, the rabbi was the last to pull me aside. Joe was busy downing Jameson with his friends and outside, under the tent, people had pulled on sweaters and were swaying to a song by Lucinda Williams. The rabbi handed me a glass of champagne. "I see Joe chose to wear the yarmulke. That was kind of him."

I nodded. Together we looked out over the crowd. There were German Baptists and Jews, atheists and Buddhists. There were Southern Baptists, Catholics, and Methodists. There were architects and farmers, furniture makers and attorneys, professors, artists, and bakers.

"You know, living out here, you must be brave," the rabbi said.

I turned to look at the rabbi, but there was little in his face to indicate whether the statement had been an observation, a blessing, or a command.

He leaned in and raised his glass. "You must be brave."

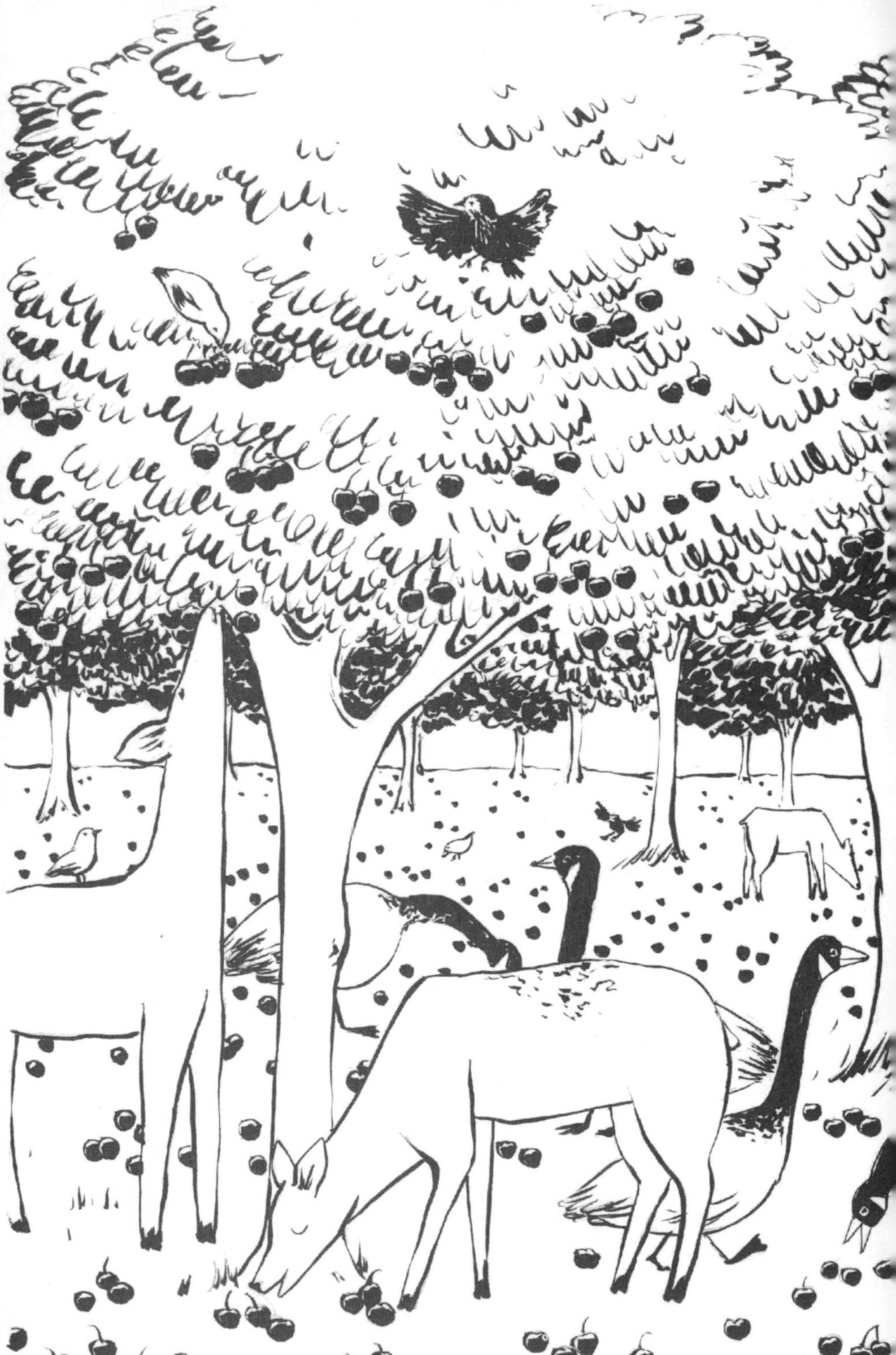

13

HARVEST

To THE COLLECTIVE relief of the entire region of West Michigan, the cherries ripened. Across the road from Replica Dodge and in orchards all along the coast, the long green leaves of those gnarled trees now hid fruit. Everyone knew it. When those leaves fluttered back in the breeze, there flashed a supreme undercoat of red.

The Mannens were known for welcoming anyone into the orchard to gather what was left after the harvest, which, James Skipton told me, had been an incredible amount of fruit in previous years. In the weeks after the wedding, the jewels ripened from peach-blush to deep scarlet. Now as the weather grew hotter and the days got as long as they were going to get, a careful glee traveled along our mile-long stretch of road. The cherries were almost in our hands, almost bursting in our mouths.

☾

ONE MORNING IN mid-July we woke to the house trembling beneath us. It was a soft tremble that made me recall what our real estate agent, Pam, had mentioned the year before: farmhouses like ours tend to settle over time.

I went outside, squinting in the sunlight. The soft tremble became a low quake under my feet. Dozens of men were at work in the orchard. Some drove flatbed trucks hauling huge steel bins of rinsed cherries, the water sloshing out in great sheets across the road. Other trucks carried empty bins and were disappearing between the long rows of trees. Everything was wet.

The cherry shaker, the mechanical luminary of the harvest and source of the quaking, was a massive farming implement. With its metal ring clasped around the trunk, its bat-like wings spread below, once turned on, it wrenched the trunk to and fro. It was violent and beautiful and I stood at the edge of the yard watching the dirt dance around my ankles. The trees rained down their fruit into the wings of the shaker.

The men worked all morning, but by noon the last of the trucks had gone. Not an hour later a murder of crows crowded in, then a doe and her two fawns, then an eagle and a flock of geese, all sharing the orchard at the same time. It was like an oasis scene where predator and prey came to quench their thirsts in a temporary peace. Later in the evening a van of Mennonites arrived, and members of the large family spread out between the trees, the children carrying buckets and the adults lugging five-gallon pails.

It was then Scruggs dashed across the road, ripping into the orchard and barking. The Mennonites had no idea of his friendliness or what a frustrating day it had been for him, witnessing the harvest from his obedient distance, and as he closed in to greet them, I could see the family scrambling to pile back into their van. I was running full speed behind him when I crossed into the Mannen orchard for the first time, hollering, scolding, trying to reassure the Mennonites that he wouldn't bite, that he was a good dog. By the time I reached him, we were deep in a row of trees and the farmhouse was out of sight. I waved and mouthed *Sorry!* to the Mennonites, who slowly climbed back out of the van with their pails.

The cherries that had escaped the wings of the shaker had been smashed by the trucks, and were now smeared across the grass. There *was* an incredible amount of fruit left, just as James had promised. When I had imagined the harvest a year ago—the harvest that had never happened—I had pictured it as a gentle process. I imagined pickers scaling the trees to garner the fruit, some Johnny Appleseed version of the real thing. The reality was far more industrial, yet somehow as I saw the cherry trees close up for the first time, I realized that they bore no signs of trauma, as if each one had not, hours earlier, been throttled at the trunk.

On their branches, fistfuls of cherries remained, eclipsed by the long leaves. This is why everyone had come and would continue to come for weeks, animals and people alike. I licked my lips, reached up, and pulled three cherries off a tree. I walked the dog home. The wait was over, the word was spreading. The harvest was here.

☾

THE DOLLAR GENERAL was empty when I arrived on a Wednesday, a month later in August. The cashier, a teenager I had seen around campus, greeted me as she continued to shelve panty hose. That afternoon I was tired, and the Dollar General was the only stop on my way home that would have what I needed. I wound my way to the back aisle that housed generic lotions, ibuprofen, blushers, tweezers, hairspray, bobby pins, tampons. And pregnancy tests.

They were almost sold out.

I glanced around to make sure I was alone. The last bright pink box had been pushed to the back of the metal shelf. "Unsurpassed accuracy!" the box boasted. I tried to envision the women who had come before me to purchase all the other boxes. Did they wear the same slack look on their faces as I did that afternoon, a fear that had run out of fuel? Were they younger or older? Did they buy one box, or two to make sure? Would they drive home in a dazed hurry to pee on the magical white wand? Would they turn away for the wait, or watch, unblinking, for the results?

It was as if the box itself possessed a tense energy that I needed to control, to contain. On the drive home I clasped the wheel in one hand and the box in the other. Purchasing it had transformed my tiredness into an uneasy alertness, and I didn't let the box go, not on the drive home, not getting out of the truck, not climbing the steps to the farmhouse or breezing past the dog, who leapt up to greet me.

I was five days late. I had never been five days late. I shut myself in the bathroom and peed. Behind me the wand sat on the top of the toilet as I studied my reflection in the mirror. Twenty-seven years old and a month married. My gold Star of David rested at my clavicle, glinting under the vanity lights, the only jewelry I wore other than my rings. Next to the wand, Joe's old digital wristwatch ticked off the passing minutes in seconds: 5:46 p.m. 5:47. 5:48.

I picked up the test and at first there was nothing but a single solid pink bar signaling a negative result. I exhaled, looked up, thanked God. Then I looked back down at the test, where right before my eyes, faint and broken, the second line appeared.

☾

WE HAD PLANNED on having children, but never this soon. Not a month after the wedding. The dog was outside the bathroom door, whining to let me know he needed to go out. I tucked the test into my back pocket, leashed the dog, and headed into the orchard.

By now, three weeks after the harvest, the orchard reeked. The remaining cherries were dropping into the grass to rot, but even as the red juice stained my slip-ons and I stopped to scratch the dog behind the ears, everything seemed miles away from my touch.

I knew exactly when I had gotten pregnant.

For several days earlier in the month, a heat wave had descended on Mason County. The barn thermometer had read eighty-eight, then ninety-seven, then over a hundred. There was zero wind.

"That does it. I'm turning on the air-conditioning," I told Joe. "At least while we're sleeping."

"I would like to invite you to sleep on top of the sheets with me. It's fine, really. It turns out you don't really need covers at night."

I rolled my eyes. Growing up in Houston meant our family's air-conditioner was flipped on in March and kept cold and blowing into September, and on top of that, the recent long cool Michigan spring had failed to prepare me for its sporadic summer pinnacle. "Are you kidding me?"

"Just wait, okay? This is Michigan. The lake always brings back the breeze. The heat will break, I promise."

But the heat didn't break. Two more days passed. On the fifth scorching day, I suddenly recalled what James had told me about our basement, that it stayed cool even during the worst heat. Though we hardly went down there, the basement of the farm-house was carpeted—"finished," as Pam had called it—and there was a sliding glass door leading out into the yard behind it. It was well lit, livable, and dry. The only drawbacks were the ubiquitous daddy longlegs, but by then I was ready to accept the trade-off. On the fifth night of the heat wave, I heaved the mattress off our bed and shoved it down the stairs.

Joe came home from the college. "Where's our bed?"

"In the only cool place in this house. Unless you want the air-conditioning on, you're going to have to sleep down there with me."

That night, the deep, cool sleep I had longed for arrived in our basement. So did our first child.

Now, returning from the orchard, I came home to find Joe's truck in the drive. He was unpacking the remainder of his lunch when I walked in.

"I was thinking of making curry tonight. Spicy or sweet?" he said.

Everything still seemed miles away from my touch. I unleashed the dog and refilled his water bowl. I told myself to wait. To wait before telling Joe, at least until my disorientation had settled down, but as soon as I was in the kitchen the news came rushing out.

"We're pregnant."

Joe stopped. He was holding a pear. Very carefully, very slowly, he put it back in the fridge. He looked at me and I tried to force a smile across my face. Then I realized there was no point. Like me, Joe was terrified.

"Are you sure?"

I placed the test between us on the counter. "I'm sure. We're going to be parents."

14

HOME

"I'm underqualified," I told Jen.

We were running the cross-country course at the edge of campus, where the cicadas sang out in the tall grasses lining the trail and the late September sun warmed my shoulders. A dim flicker of anticipation pumped through my body. My doctor had confirmed the pregnancy a few days earlier.

"It's as if I've been given a target, but no landmarks. I'm not prepared. What if the baby has Down syndrome? What if I gain four hundred pounds? What if I hate being a mom? Kids always kind of annoyed me, even when I was a kid."

Jen laughed. "Let's walk for a moment."

"And I have no idea what Joe is thinking. He's become even quieter, if that's possible."

"Well, think about the news in Joe's brain. He's trying to understand a complex equation but he can't. Neither can you, which makes you two smart people with zero answers. Unfortunately, that's parenthood. There's no solving the complexities beforehand. Like everyone else you learn by doing." Jen smiled. "But you are qualified."

"Do you know what I realized the other day?" I stopped. "I realized that the only other Jew in Mason County is right here, inside of me. Until they grow up and decide to convert, which they probably will." I took a long drink of water. "Probably I'm pregnant with a Lutheran."

"We already have lots of Lutherans around here." Jen picked up speed again. "What we need are more Jews."

☾

FOR MUCH OF history Judaism has been a matrilineal religion, which means that if the mother is Jewish, the child is Jewish, even if the father is not. Some decades ago my own branch of Judaism, Reform, adopted a bilineal policy stating that if either parent is Jewish, the child is a Jew. And, I kept reminding myself, they would be raised that way.

Two more weeks passed and Art Thigpen returned to Replica Dodge, his truck full of cut wood and juvenile delinquents. The days were still long but the mornings were beginning to pocket some bite. The green herons had recently left for Mexico. As I watched the men unload the wood, the cut logs smacking onto the concrete again, I had the keen sense of reliving the same moment from the previous year. The grand pile was accumulating again, all that oak to be stacked and burned through winter. Only now, everything was different.

We had seen the child's heartbeat at the ultrasound, a cluster of bright pulsating pixels. We had seen the child move, looking more like a squirrel than a human, pitching around in its canoe-shaped womb.

Joe had started setting his alarm earlier and showering every morning of the week.

"You've never showered this much," I commented one morning. "Normal people do. But not you."

"It's time I start looking like a professional at the college. I mean, I'm still wearing the same clothes I did in graduate school."

I smiled. "So you want to go buy some fine menswear this weekend?"

Joe's serious answer took me by surprise. "Well, at least some dress shirts," he murmured.

For weeks I had been trying to give Joe the mental space I thought he needed. Long periods of peering into his binoculars on the porch, long walks around the property at dusk. He always invited me to go with him, and I often did, but I kept any impulse to litter those moments with extraneous speech in check. I tried to keep the conversation light, because everything I knew about Joe told me that Jen was right. Like me, Joe was trying to meticulously piece together the unknowable future.

One afternoon he arrived home with a chalkboard, big enough for an entire classroom, in his truck bed. It was old but in excellent condition. He called me out to help him move it inside. I stood at the tailgate. "Where did you get this?"

"Online from a local seller. Don't worry, it wasn't expensive."

"It's beautiful. Just a little unexpected."

"Don't you think we'll need it? I mean eventually. Eventually we'll need to teach them things."

Dear God. Joe was frantically trying to wrap his head around becoming a parent, but so far he had only reached the point of understanding the child as an extension of his work as an educator. I felt for him. This was far greater than any classroom experiment, but for all he knew, we were about to inherit our ultimate student.

No, I kept thinking. We are about to *become* the students.

☾

BECAUSE OF THE sheer physicality of it, the pregnancy was a far more intimate experience for me. At the college I drifted in and out of conversations with students and colleagues, often losing focus because I was so intrigued by the tiny parasitic creature growing inside me.

One body, two heartbeats.

You must be brave, the rabbi had said.

On Rosh Hashanah, Joe picked some criterion apples and brought them inside to me. "L'shanah Tovah," he said. "Don't we need to drizzle these with honey?"

We had agreed to begin "keeping Shabbat," or observing the Sabbath, at Replica Dodge, and this would be our first. Services were out of the question, but we reasoned we could at least host a weekly Seder, or Shabbat meal, at the farmhouse. In the year since moving in, I had never attempted to prepare one. I feared it would seem anemic without the company of other Jews and, like cleaning for Passover, I also worried that I wouldn't do things right.

Yet something about the pregnancy forced me to forge ahead. I memorized the Shabbat blessings, and I decorated our table with the china we had received as wedding gifts. I cut fresh flowers in the yard and arranged them in a vase. I placed the challah plate in the middle of the table beside the flowers. There was no congregation, but we had each other and the child. At sundown, as the room dimmed, I lit the Shabbat candles and repeated the Hebrew blessing. *Baruch atah, Adonai Eloheinu, melech haolam, asher kid'shanu b'mitzvotav, v'tzivanu l'hadlik ner shel Shabbat.* Then we kissed and ate in the warm dark of the room.

It was a tradition I vowed to continue after the child was born, but despite the sweetness of celebrating our first Shabbat together, my doubts loomed large.

Was it even possible to raise a Jewish kid in Mason County? How would we cultivate that Jewish identity in someone who would rarely see evidence of the religion beyond their own home?

With no local community, how would they associate Judaism with anything but the bitter sting of being left out? Especially at Christmas. How would we navigate the holiday season? And what about the soft persuasion of well-meaning Christians, or worse, those fired up about hell? In Replica Dodge, in the rolling hills of West Michigan, was it even possible to raise a child who would be proud to be a Jew?

At this point in the season we could smell the concord grapes as soon as we stepped outside. The vines were almost as old as the house itself, and for over a hundred years they had grown in that small sunlit patch behind the back door. They were brittle and peeling with age, but each fall they produced their spherical wonders in abundance. One Friday afternoon in late September, hours before the Seder, Joe went out to the arbor and filled a five-gallon bucket with them.

He came back inside to wash and pick them over. Going over each bunch, he tossed out the imperfect grapes, the green ones, and those already gone soft. That afternoon as I watched him work, I realized there was no point in speaking my doubts out loud. Joe knew them. He mashed the grapes and boiled them in water. He stretched a sieve over the biggest bowl we owned and poured the hot mixture over, slowly, in this way separating the flesh from the juice.

He was trying to prove that a Jewish life was possible here. Not just for me but for our child. Joe was making the Shabbat wine for that night's Seder. It was juice, really, but juice from grapes that I could see outside the window from my place at the table. After saying the blessings, I took a drink from the kiddush cup. It was thick, sweet, and had a tart aftertaste. It was the best thing I had ever tasted.

I looked back out the window, over the arbor and the barn and the hardwoods, and an astounding sadness struck me. Not because I had come to Replica Dodge, but at the thought of leaving it.

☾

ONCE WE CLEARED the first trimester, Joe and I announced the pregnancy to coworkers and friends, men who vigorously shook Joe's hand and women who squeezed me, proclaiming, "Look at you! You're already glowing!"

At first it was a relief to have the news go public, joy being almost as cumbersome as fear, but then strange things started happening. Coworkers would check out my stomach before looking up to greet me in passing. Then someone remarked that I "didn't even look pregnant." I noticed the edge in her voice, something approximating contempt. I had the singular feeling that my body was being scrutinized by everyone: by doctors, by other mothers, by former students, by strangers.

"Take some time with Joe," my mother urged. "It will be almost impossible once the baby is born. Go away together."

Our colleagues were similarly full of advice. "Bank your sleep in the coming months," they said, as if such a thing were actually possible. "Soon you won't be getting any."

We were inundated with unsolicited advice about every aspect of parenting. People encouraged us to immerse the child in the arts and avoid full-contact sports. They told us to be parents to our kids, not friends with them. That week at work I kept noticing my zipper was open, that my underwear was showing. Baffled, I chalked it up to an alarming wave of forgetfulness until I noticed that every time I sat in a chair, thanks to my new belly, pop! Down went my zipper. Then later that day, at my hair appointment in Ludington, my stylist described the afternoon her daughter was almost kidnapped by "a fat man at the mall."

I grappled with this new universe of conversations I had unwittingly entered. Everyone spoke to me as if we had known each other for years. These conversations went against everything I had learned about rural Michigan culture so far: its emphasis on self-containment, reliance, and soft-spokenness, on suggestion rather than statement. Somehow the subject of parenthood superseded those boundaries. It was dizzying.

"This your first?" a nurse asked me, coming into my room at the doctor's office.

I nodded.

"Oh, I know all your new-mom fears." She took my blood pressure. "But don't worry. The vagina is a magnificent accordion, expanding at birth and healing tight again."

I turned away so she wouldn't see my mouth hanging open. How was this, also, Michigan?

By then it was October and on my morning runs—slower now—the dog and I met hunters tracking deer or dragging bloodied-mouth bucks from the woods. I nodded and waved, the sight no longer a surprise. I returned to the farmhouse, usually, to discover a package on the porch from my mother full of newborn clothes. And I would sit there, panting from the run, thumbing the fabric of the tiny pajamas, the socks and hats, trying to visualize the child who would wear them.

Among the litany of questions people asked—When are you due? Do you know the baby's gender? Do you have a name picked out? Will you breastfeed? Where will the baby sleep? When will you return to work?—what nobody asked me was how I was planning to raise a Jewish kid in Mason County.

The child's spiritual future was, however, on at least one other person's mind. One morning I came back from a run to find a package that was not from my mother but from an acquaintance. I opened the gift-wrapped box. Inside was a single item: *Two from Galilee: The Story of Mary and Joseph*, by Marjorie Holmes ("The Greatest Love Story of All," the cover boasted). The book was short and light and I leafed through its pages, skimming some paragraphs before closing it.

The woman knew I was Jewish. I flirted with the idea that the gift was an attempt at an interfaith dialogue, and I wondered if I should send her *Tales of the Hasidim* or *Honey from the Rock* in return. Far more likely, this was her Christian attempt to tap me on the shoulder, and it reminded me of an old Jewish joke.

Two elderly women gather at the synagogue to prepare for Shabbat.

"What do you call the grandchildren of an interfaith couple?" one asks the other.

"That's easy," says the other woman. "Christians."

I decided to take my mother's advice and get away.

☾

THE STORY OF *Mary and Joseph* gave me the overwhelming urge to return to any city. Fast. I needed six lanes of traffic swirling around me, a sidewalk swarming with people. A place where no one knew my name.

"We could go over winter break," I told Joe that night.

"I thought we were going to my parents' house for Christmas."

"To celebrate Christmas? Is this something we'll be doing after our Jewish child is born? Celebrating Christmas at your parents' place?"

"Christmas doesn't matter to me. You know that. Seeing family does."

"Can we take this year off?"

Joe spit his toothpaste into the sink. "Where do you want to go instead?"

I turned on the faucet. "Chicago."

"Who do we know in Chicago?"

"No one. Joe, I just have to get out of here."

"For now? Or for good?"

The baby started to kick. I put my toothbrush back in its cup.

"I'm saying we should go and try to figure some things out."

☾

ON THE FRIGID Monday before Christmas we made it to the outskirts of Chicago and sat in traffic for another two hours. I had almost forgotten that experience, traffic. The slow parade of red taillights weaving in and out, the semi that kept ratcheting to a stop six inches from our back bumper. If not for the temperature, which hovered right around zero, I could close my eyes, sink into the honking, and almost believe I was back in Houston.

That winter was off to a fierce start, and by then the media had branded it with a new catchphrase. They called it the "polar vortex." "Polar vortex" cluttered newsreels nationwide, though I could never figure out exactly what the phrase meant. It seemed to mean different things in different parts of the country. In Michigan the polar vortex meant that any time it warmed up to above twenty degrees, another system of gusting whiteouts, single-digit temperatures, and subzero wind chills was already making its way down from Canada.

On the Monday evening we arrived at our rented condo in the Ukrainian Village northwest of downtown, Chicago was in the midst of the coldest temperatures the city had seen in the last decade. But the polar vortex held little sway over the people of Chicago. Though the snow quieted the streets, the city moved just as fast, and each morning of that week, Joe and I would leave our rented condo to walk the Ukrainian Village, bundled like pipes to prevent freezing. We made our careful way over the ice, passing Roberto Clemente High School, and stopped to admire the Serbian Orthodox Church.

Two days later at the Field Museum we paid good money to see an exhibit on bioluminescence, but I kept finding the children in attendance far more fascinating. In the grand foyer I watched three girls in black hijabs chase one another around Carl Akeley's famous elephants, the littlest of them always a step behind her sisters. Then in the darkness of the exhibit, I watched a young family standing in the soft green glow of a firefly model, their son having rushed ahead, his face pressed hard against a fish tank, awaiting that sudden flicker of some creature of light.

Would our lives be better here? Would they be easier? Now that I was back in a booming metropolis, could I say, definitively, one way or the other?

What did I want for this child—a Jewish identity no matter what? There was a *mezuzah* on the doorpost of our condo and symbols of a thriving Jewish presence emerged at every corner. There was Manny's Coffee Shop and Deli, the Jewish Theological Seminary downtown, and the stoic Chicago Loop Synagogue. On Christmas Day we dined at Ras Dashen, an Ethiopian restaurant, *injera* sponge bread soaking up the spiced red lentils, our mouths wonderfully ablaze. Nobody wished us a Merry Christmas.

I fully expected Chicago to strengthen the hunch I had upon first moving to Replica Dodge. Mason County was just a stopover, an obstacle to overcome on the road to life in more suitable locales. Relocating had always been a *when* to me, not an *if*. Maybe not to the Windy City, but somewhere, and all week I tried to picture it, living in Chicago—or Austin, Portland, New York, Miami—somewhere a Jewish community would be a built-in reality rather than some curious homespun marvel. All week I waited for Chicago, in every delicious experience the freezing city held forth to me, to grant me that clean break.

I wanted to forget Replica Dodge, our farmhouse, the red barn.

Instead the opposite happened. As I stood in front of the condo's dinky computerized thermostat, I was reminded of the good full heat of the farmhouse's woodstove. Remembering stacking wood with Joe instinctively made me smile. Then later, slipping off to sleep, another image came to me: the dog running leashless at twilight, ripping through the hardwoods, picking up the scent of some doe he would never catch. The next morning I woke from a dream similar to the one I had had months before. My hand open under the sun, in it a fistful of cherries gleaming.

In Chicago Joe had been trying hard not to seem exquisitely out of place. Crowded out, rattled by the sirens howling past our window at night, by the taxis that would change lanes without warning, by the throngs that shoved into the tiny elevator with us at the Shakespeare Theater. There was love in his pretending, but I spotted it as pretense a mile away. By Friday morning, as we packed our bags to leave, Joe fell ill. Within a few hours he vomited three times and I watched as the color drained from his face.

Certainly there was a physical cause for his sudden affliction, but it also seemed indicative of internalized stress. I knew Joe feared he would ultimately wind up in a place like this. Some boisterous metropolis overrun with people, bare of hardwoods, where there would be no acres, no land. For Joe that meant no peace.

We gathered our suitcases, tidied up the condo, and packed the car, and Joe eased into the passenger seat. We exited the Ukrainian Village, navigated through downtown, then merged back onto I-94, this time westward bound. Now there was no traffic. A radio announcer came on to say that the latest storm of the polar vortex was heading for Michigan.

At seventy-five miles an hour, we were chasing it down.

Though the coldest winter in the last decade had failed to obscure Chicago's enchantments, in the end, I discovered there was nothing permanent about the city for me. Our visit had been a temporary escape—a needed one—but I didn't want to stay. Behind the wheel I began planning our menu for that night's Shabbat Seder in Replica Dodge. I thought about the storm. I should have felt scared, but I didn't. We were going home.

☾

I THOUGHT I knew how this book would end.

Here's what I was going to write. Unlike the house and barn, no matter how proudly it once stood, Bill Broadwell's bizarre western tribute town would disintegrate in the next few polar vortex winters. Signs of demise were everywhere. The wood of the barbershop was beginning to rot. The floors in the Long Branch Saloon were riddled with rodent nests. Replica Dodge wasn't built to last.

This slow crumbling of Bill's city would hold a mirror up to my own revelation. To survive, at least spiritually speaking, I would need to leave Mason County, and in doing so, I would finally become a good Jew, get out of the woods, and go join my people. One must choose, I had planned to write, between the land and the tribe.

Here's the problem with plans: life happens. At twenty weeks along, after another lengthy ultrasound, we received a report describing our child as "an unremarkable fetus." This was medical-speak, the doctor explained, for no abnormalities detected. No cleft lip, all limbs present, no early signs of Down syndrome. Each of the four chambers of the heart was pumping just as it should. The child's brain was lit up in all the usual places, its head measurement was within a normal range. Its spine was sheathed and properly connecting the brain to the body.

The child twisted and leaned in the womb, and we held our breath. For several minutes, the technician kept waving her wand up my abdomen with increasing pressure, trying to identify the sex. The child kept moving away, crossing its legs. Finally the technician caught a glimpse and announced, "I think you're having a girl. I think. I could be wrong."

The likelihood that our daughter would be born healthy, with no major cognitive disability, and full term, with lungs capable of taking air, was good, yet the possibility that at any point her heart would stop beating somehow still seemed close at hand. Our fears lingered. The first report on our daughter was long and positive, but it only said what was, not what would be.

Now she kicks and hiccups and flips over several times a day, and whenever anything is placed on my stomach—a hand or the binding of a book—she kneads her shoulder against it. I smile, knowing her strength, if yet not her face.

Although leaving Mason County once seemed like the only ending I could write, it now seems dishonest to try to pinpoint where Joe and I will be in five years. These days we're renovating a room of the farmhouse, ripping up carpet. We're building a nursery for her, reinsulating the space so she'll be warm in the upcoming Michigan winters.

A week ago we spoke to Joe's mother on the phone. We described the annual Hanukkah celebration we would host at Replica Dodge. This was me actively creating space, which I knew I would have to do, again and again, as long as I lived in Mason County.

It was fine until I began to notice how quiet the telephone line had become. Maybe Joe's mother had been suspecting this for years, after Joe stopped attending Mass as a teenager, and definitely later, when he showed up in a yarmulke at his wedding. Still here it was for the first time, spoken. Her tradition ended, ours begun. In a few decades' time, who could say that the same wouldn't happen to me? Would our daughter call me, one random Thursday, to let me know of her plans to raise her own children in some other faith?

Maybe that's more likely to occur if we stay here, without a temple, in this land of German Baptists and two-tracks, fruit farms, roadkill, and rifle season. But for now we are home.

There's so much I don't know about the future, but this much seems undeniable. There is a dark sapphire of a girl coming who will know how to build a fire, like her father. She will know the Friday evening blessings said over the candles, like her mother. She will whisper the *Sh'ma* before bedtime, and on some bright mornings, she will follow her father into the hardwoods, into his own house of worship, field guide in hand.

Someday maybe she will tear down this thin dirt road on the back of an Appaloosa, full speed ahead, reins held taut, her straight hair whipping around her slender face. I don't know if she will embrace Judaism, but she will have a Jewish name. She will be named Rivka. Rivka from *ribbaq*, meaning to tie together, to ensnare, to bind.

I can't say what will happen to Replica Dodge. It's true it won't last, but disassembling Bill's buildings, the schoolhouse and the saloon, the general store and the Lady's Emporium, and selling the antiques as Pam suggested, years ago now, doesn't seem a befitting finale for the little western town built among the cherry trees. Whatever happens, something tells me that we'll be here, like loved ones, to witness the end of Replica Dodge.

Of the end, a great Jewish master, Rabbi Zusya of Hanipol, once wrote: *In the coming world, they will not ask me, "Why were you not Moses?" They will ask me, "Why were you not Zusya?"*

And so these are the only final lines I can write, that as much as Jews are known for sticking together, they are also well-documented pioneers. And if Mason County has taught me anything, it's that all it means to be a pioneer is to enter the wilderness and make something of it. Despite everything. Despite everything: this is the Jewish story. In strange new lands Jews have survived, are surviving, and will survive, in some moments merely dragging on, but in others dashing forward.

ACKNOWLEDGMENTS

PARENTS SACRIFICE A bewildering amount in their efforts to raise strong, kind, and resourceful kids. The sheer number of people doing this work, every day, all over the world, continues to astonish me, but good parenting is not a given. It's a godsend.

When I showed an early interest in writing my parents could have said, "It will make you no money." They could have said, "No one reads much anymore." They could have nudged me into more normal activities for kids my age, like soccer or gymnastics.

Instead they hired a writing coach, a young professor named Lisa Golding, who buzzed up to our house each Wednesday afternoon in her fire-red Mustang, took my writing seriously, and came to epitomize what a life working with words *can* look like—not the starving artist, but the free and bold and professional version. Later that year, Lisa and my parents organized a reading for me and staged it in our living room. No, I'm not kidding. Yes, I wore a beret.

My parents saw who I was, a writer—and later a Jew—and chose to honor these emerging identities rather than run from them. This is some of the hardest work good parents do. Thank you, Mom and Dad.

On that note: when Annie Martin first contacted me about this project, my son, our second child, was three months old. I was spending most of my nights on the couch, sleeping sitting up, Linus on my chest. He refused to sleep anywhere else, he nursed around the clock, and between running after Rivka during the day and feeding Linus all night, I did not feel free and bold and professional. Then Annie called. Another godsend.

Thank you to the wonderful women at Wayne State University Press: Annie Martin, Carrie Teefey, Rachel Ross, Emily Nowak, and Robin DuBlanc, queen of copyediting.

Early readers of this fledgling manuscript included Erin Blakeslee, Nathan Lipps, the novelist Jon Sealy (*The Whiskey Baron*), Professor Seán Henne, and author Joni Rodgers, all of whom challenged me, in various ways, to tell the real story. A special thanks goes to Erin, who encouraged me to explore my conversion rather than brush past it, and to Jon, who told me not to give up.

This project had several champions, but arguably no one was more in my corner writing-wise than my longtime friend and mentor, Joni Rodgers. With her pull-no-punches approach to constructive criticism (which she somehow manages to deliver with equal parts joie de vivre and loving-kindness), Joni saw this book from the finish line as I struggled through the middle miles, and her expertise about the industry and the book itself became invaluable. Currently Joni runs Westport Lighthouse Writers Retreat in Washington State, and if your writing is floundering, I encourage you to check that option out. Thank you, Joni.

Thank you to Emily Joynton, whose genius high-graphic illustrations completed this project. They say don't hire family, but I say hire family you can count on. Emily's vision, skill, and follow-through transformed this project in positive ways I couldn't even anticipate beforehand, and for that I am eternally grateful.

The Mason County District Library and the people who work there also deserve special note here. Actually, they deserve much more than that. Most of this book was written in a little room dedicated to local history at the library. Thank you to Directors Sue Carlson and Eric Smith, who opened up that room for me whenever I came to write, and to Emily Garland, Katie McPike, Tami Sturgill, and Patti Skinner (and Sue again!), who always make my children feel safe and loved, and in doing so help to create an environment that celebrates reading. Thank you to Liz Sterling, who has worked mightily to diversify the children's literature available to kids in Mason County.

In many ways the small college I work for feels like a big family. As uneasy as I was about staying here, the faculty and staff at West Shore Community College wrapped their arms around us—and I must say that here, Joe reminds me that the midwestern hug is an endangered species—but truly, they have supported us, loved us, and helped us call Mason County home. Our deepest gratitude to Paul and Jennifer Lundberg Anders, Carolyn and Seán Henne, Paul and Laura Drelles, Buffy and Mike Nagle, and John Wolff and Tandy Sturgeon. An additional shout-out goes to Mike Nagle, who repeatedly encouraged me to reach out to Wayne State University Press.

Joe. You are my match and my teammate, and I love you. Thank you for watching the kids while I write this.

By the way, I agree. The answers are out there.

ABOUT THE AUTHOR

NATALIE RUTH JOYNTON's work has appeared in *American Poetry Review, Michigan Quarterly,* and *Poetry International.* She is the recipient of the 2010 Scholl/Thompson Poetry Prize from the Academy of American Poets as well as a Quintilian Excellence in Teaching Award from Purdue University, where she earned her MFA in creative writing. Natalie lives, writes, and teaches in rural West Michigan. This is her first book. Learn more at natalieruthjoynton.com.

ABOUT THE ILLUSTRATOR

EMILY JOYNTON IS a freelance illustrator based in Philadelphia. She has worked professionally with the Chicago-based band Wilco and the Maryland Institute College of Art, where she earned an MFA in illustration practice in 2017. Emily has published several short personal narrative comics and is currently working on a collection of unique greeting cards. To see more of Emily's illustration work, visit www.automaticbizooty.com.